TERENCE PETER CROSBY

GW00601575

My book of Hobbies and God's book, the Bible

DayOne

© Day One Publications 2006
First printed 2006

ISBN 1 84625 024 -2

9 781846 250248

Published by Day One Publications
Ryelands Road, Leominster, HR6 8NZ
☎ 01568 613 740 FAX 01568 611 473
email—sales@dayone.co.uk
web site—www.dayone.co.uk
North American—e-mail—sales@dayonebookstore.com
North American—web site—www.dayonebookstore.com

Illustrations by Brad Goodwin
Designed by Steve Devane and printed by Gutenberg Press, Malta

Contents

Dedication

To Brian and Ulrike Warner
In gratitude for their friendship and fellowship
at The Cornerstone Christian Bookshop,
Clapham Junction

D r Crosby's enthusiasm for life and the Bible permeate the pages of this fascinating book. His broad range of interests coupled with fine interpretive skills should not only delight readers, but also encourage Bible teachers to be wide ranging in their application of scriptural truths.

Like one of his great heroes Charles Haddon Spurgeon, Terence Crosby has drawn on numerous subjects. Spurgeon wrote about the way illustrations can be gathered from a variety of sources and commended the use of: 'Current history, newspapers, ancient history, religious history, and the natural world.'

Readers of this fine volume will likewise find ample to stimulate their minds, by being encouraged to look *down* at worms and leeches, then to look *around* at steam engines, cathedrals and cricket, while not forgetting to enjoy a nice cup of tea on their travels!

Look down, look around but also look *up*, for the book is topped and tailed with the heavens above and the heaven to come.

Enjoy this rich fare and may God be pleased to bless these pages to many people.

Clive Anderson
The Butts Church, Alton
April 2006

Introduction

For many years most of the congregation at Trinity Road Chapel in South London have gone away on Church Camp for a week. As one who has never had any wish to go camping, I've always been among the few left behind every August and it became a tradition for me to be asked to be the preacher on these occasions! One year I decided to speak about one of my hobbies and to show what it taught about ourselves and about God. Having done it once, it seemed a good idea to do it again—and again! The Lord Jesus Christ often taught the people by means of illustrations and parables; picture-language can make things come alive and help us to understand them better. In this book I've rearranged my hobby sermons to fit in with the thoughts of the man who wrote Proverbs 30 in the Old Testament, a man of many interests. I haven't tried to follow his thoughts and words exactly, but have used them to introduce my own hobbies and interests to you. Without doubt some of them (and hopefully many) will be things that you already enjoy yourself. You may even find yourself picking up a new hobby or interest! But most of all, I trust that you'll pick up many precious and important truths from the Bible which will be a great help to you.

Terence Peter Crosby
Wandsworth, London

The mastermind

What are your favourite hobbies and interests? I'm sure you must have some! In the following chapters we're going to look at some of my interests and find out what the Bible teaches about them and what they teach us about the Bible. But first I want to introduce you to a very interesting man who is going to help us on our way. You've heard of King David who wrote most of the Psalms; you've heard of David's son, King Solomon, who wrote most of the Proverbs. But if you turn in your Bible to Proverbs chapter 30, you will find that it was written by another man, 'Agur the son of Jakeh' (v.1). And that's all we know about him! But as we look through his chapter we can learn a lot about his character. I think you'll agree that he was a very clever man, a good thinker, someone who kept his eyes open and who was very interested in the things going on around him in God's creation. He was also a man who respected God and who had a good understanding of God's word. But let's find out what he has to say about himself—and it may come as a bit of a shock!

Agur's view of self

Surely I am more stupid than any man, and do not have the understanding of a man. I neither learned wisdom nor have knowledge of the Holy One (vv.2–3).

Some people talk like that without meaning it, but Agur meant every word. When he thought about God, the great and 'Holy One', Agur felt very small. He goes on to ask some very deep questions—'Who has ascended into heaven, or descended? Who has gathered the wind in his fists? Who has bound the waters in a garment? Who has established all the ends of the earth? What is his name, and what is his Son's name, if you know?' (v.4).

Agur had to confess that he didn't know the answers. The deeds of God are far too wonderful for a mere man to explain fully. Agur would agree with the words of David, 'Such knowledge is too wonderful for me' (Psalm 139:6). How different to many people today who make out that they are so clever; they would have us believe that they know everything! But the big difference is that they do not know the God who made them. Agur did. Do you sometimes feel proud of yourself and think that others ought to praise you? Because of our disobedience to God we all get like that at times. The Bible puts us in our place.

Listen to what the apostle Paul wrote to some churches—he told everyone 'not to think of himself more highly than he ought to think' (Romans 12:3). 'And if anyone thinks that he knows anything, he knows nothing yet as he ought to know' (1 Corinthians 8:2). 'For if anyone thinks himself to be something, when he is nothing, he deceives himself' (Galatians 6:3). What good company Agur was in! We can speak highly about him, but it was to his credit that he could speak humbly about himself. In fact he was obeying one of the proverbs of Solomon in an earlier chapter—'Let another man praise you, and not your own mouth; a stranger, and not your own lips' (Proverbs 27:2).

Next, in complete contrast, Agur speaks very highly indeed about something completely different.

Agur's view of Scripture

Every word of God is pure; he is a shield to those who put their trust in him. Do not add to his words, lest he rebuke you, and you be found a liar (vv. 5–6).

Agur wanted to praise God and God's Word and here he teaches us two important lessons about God's Word. We can rely on it to be completely true and there is absolutely no need to add anything to it. Isn't the Bible a wonderful book? And isn't it a wonderful thing that we can trust in God, its author, to be our protector?

But Agur also warns us to take God's Word seriously and not to fool around with it. Don't be misled by people who may tell you that you can't believe in Genesis or the miracles of Jesus or the resurrection or many other important truths about God and about yourself. God knows better than these people do. The whole of his word is true. And beware of people who want to add to the Bible. They may tell you that you have to do certain things to be right with God; if these things are not in the Bible, don't take any notice. They may hand you another book which they say is more important than the Bible; don't bother with it. They may make out that God has told them something special that he has left out of his word. Just remember what Agur said—'Do not add to his words'. Are you glad and excited that you've got God's very own word in your very own Bible? Remember how God expects us to treat his word—'You shall not add to the word which I command you, nor take from it, that you may keep the commandments of the LORD your God which I command you' (Deuteronomy 4:2).

When we read God's Word we learn about the things God hates; if we love God we ought to love the things he loves and hate the things he hates. Agur thought like that. God hates sin, so Agur hated sin and he was afraid of falling into sin. The next part of his chapter is a prayer to God about this.

Agur's view of sin

How well do you know the Ten Commandments? Agur knew them very well and reminds us of a few of them. How well do you know the Lord's Prayer? Agur didn't know it—he lived centuries before the Lord Jesus Christ—but in his prayer he even has some of the same thoughts as those that would be in the Lord's Prayer. See if you can spot the connections:

- 'Remove falsehood and lies far from me' (v.8); 'You shall not bear false witness against your neighbour' (Exodus 20:16). Ask God to help you not to tell lies.
- 'Give me neither poverty nor riches—feed me with the food allotted to me ...' (v.8); 'Give us this day our daily bread' (Matthew 6:11). God knows exactly what you need. Ask him to give you that, just that.
- '... lest I be full and deny you, and say, "Who is the LORD?" Or lest I be poor and steal' (v.9); 'You shall not steal ...' (Exodus 20:15). Ask God to help you never to steal something that doesn't belong to you.
- '... and profane the name of my God' (v.9); 'You shall not take the name of the LORD your God in vain' (Exodus 20:7). 'Our Father in heaven, hallowed be Your name' (Matthew 6:9). Ask God to help you not to do or say things which dishonour his name.

Agur certainly knew how to pray, didn't he? We could sum up his prayer in the words of the Lord's Prayer—'And do not lead us into temptation, but deliver us from the evil one' (Matthew 6:13).

In the next few verses Agur has some more of the Ten Commandments on his mind. He speaks of 'a generation that curses its father, and does not bless its mother' (v.11) and of the 'eye that mocks his father, and scorns obedience to his mother' (v.17), which ought to remind us of the commandment 'Honour your father and your mother' (Exodus 20:12). Ask God to help you show proper respect to your parents. Agur even refers to people who commit adultery and who are unfaithful to their marriage-partners, reminding us that God said 'You shall not commit adultery' (Exodus 20:14).

Perhaps you feel that you don't need to ask God to protect you from doing something as horrible as that, or from something as awful as murdering somebody. Perhaps you don't think that you have ever lied or stolen something or dishonoured your parents or God's name. There are plenty of people who would say that they don't sin. Read carefully what Agur says about them. He describes them as 'a generation that is pure in its own eyes, yet is not washed from its filthiness' (v.12).

You may think that you are good and even religious, but it's what God says about us that counts, not what we say about ourselves. The apostle Paul tells us that 'all have sinned and fall short of the glory of God' (Romans 3:23). Agur knew that included him, and it includes you and me as well. The Lord Jesus Christ came to this earth and died on the cross not to save those people who are too proud to own up to God about their sin, but to forgive and save those who would own up and pray 'God be merciful to me a sinner' (Luke 18:13). That's why some very bad people who have done some terrible things get saved and go to heaven, while lots of very good religious people don't own up to being sinners and never get forgiven. What about you?

As we close this chapter written by Agur, we're going to see another side to his character. So far we've heard him talking about self, Scripture and sin.

Agur's view of science and society

You may have been told that Christians are boring killjoys. Don't you believe it! Christians have to be serious about serious things, as Agur was, but Agur had his eyes open. He was wide awake. He looked around at God's creation and enjoyed it. He was 'with it' in the best possible sense! So many things seemed to interest him—the elements (fire, earth, water) in verse 16, transport (ships) in verse 19, as well as all different kinds of people (servants, kings, fools, husbands, wives, and so on).

But his great hobby seems to have been zoology. He almost takes us on a guided tour of the zoo (or, if you don't approve of zoos, what about the wildlife park?). First we peep into the Aquarium, I imagine. Agur shows us the leech (v.15), that worm which sucks blood—a bit creepy, but doctors have found it very useful! Next Agur takes us to the Birds of Prey Aviaries for a spot of bird-watching. Do you remember what Jesus said? 'Look at the birds of the air' (Matthew 6:26). First we see the ravens and young eagles being fed (v.17). Then we are treated to a special display of falconry and we observe 'the way of an eagle in the air' (v.19). 'Isn't that a wonderful sight?' exclaims Agur. Now we're whisked off to the Reptile House to see 'the way of a serpent on a rock' (v.19). 'Amazing!' says our guide.

Then he's off again, leading us round some of the other animal houses in search of some small but wise creatures. In the Insect House we observe ants preparing for the winter (v.25), locusts on the march (v.27) and some spiders (v.28)—if you use a Bible version other than the New King James you may need to go back to the Reptile House at this point to see some lizards instead of the spiders; the Small Mammal House includes a group of rock badgers hiding in the rocks (v.26). We'll visit these small wise creatures in another chapter when we've got more time.

But for now we'll make do with a quick look at the lions (v.30)—again, we'll come back to the big cats in another chapter—and pay a visit to the Children's Zoo where we see a greyhound and a male goat (v.31). Agur's whistle-stop guided tour is at an end.

However, just before he leaves us, Agur has what we might call 'a sting in the tail'. Are you ready for it? 'If you have been foolish in exalting yourself, or if you have devised evil, put your hand on your mouth' (v.32). What can he mean? I think he must be reminding us of what he said about himself at the start. He said he was ignorant, not wise. Now he's asking you and me if we have been foolish and proud.

Foolish people say in their hearts 'There is no God' (Psalm 14:1). Is that what you think to yourself? Foolish people boast that they are pure and clean, when God sees them as disobedient sinners. Agur tells us to cover up our mouths, because we haven't got anything about which we can boast to God. We've all thought, said and done evil, sinful things. God's Ten Commandments show up the bad things we have all done.

Can you see yourself as one who has sinned against God? Can you see that you can do nothing to put things right again? If you can, good, because there's great hope for you. God sent his son, the Lord Jesus Christ, into this world to die for sinners, to take their place and to suffer the punishment they deserve for their sin. God wants you to 'call upon him. For "whoever calls on the name of the LORD shall be saved"' (Romans 10:12–13). Pray to God, own up to him about your sin, trust in the Lord Jesus Christ to save you, and he will. Remember what Agur said about God, the One whose word is true and who keeps his promises—'He is a shield to those who put their trust in him' (v.5).

The sky at night

At the start of the chapter he wrote in the Bible (Proverbs 30:4), Agur asked a series of very hard questions which even he couldn't really answer. Do you remember what they were? The first question went like this—'Who has ascended into heaven, or descended?' He wasn't thinking about astronauts in rockets—in his time, flying was unknown. No, Agur was thinking about the great deeds of God and the wonder of God's creation. Quite likely he often looked up into the sky at night and praised God for all he could see.

One man who certainly was a bit of an astronomer was King David and you will see why if you turn to one of his psalms, which he begins by speaking to God about his glory—'O LORD, our Lord, how excellent is your name in all the earth, who have set your glory above the heavens!' (Psalm 8:1).

Do you take time to think about God and his greatness? How does it make you feel? We've seen already that it made Agur feel small and humble. It appears to have had the same effect upon David. He seems to stop and ask himself, 'But what about me? How do I fit into the big picture?' This is what he actually wrote—'When I consider your heavens, the work of your fingers, the moon and the stars, which you have ordained, what is man that you are mindful of him, and the son of man that you visit him?' (Psalm 8:3–4). David's basic question for us to answer is 'When I consider … what is man … that you visit him?'

My considering—'When I consider'

Long before he became king, David worked as a shepherd-boy. He saw a lot of the night sky and was used to looking up at the stars. This was something of which he never grew tired. Do you ever look up at the night sky? When was the last time you did it? You don't need to be a great astronomer to do that! Let's get away from all the bright lights of the city and join David in the open fields around Bethlehem where we can look up into the clear sky with him. What can we see? With David we see the heavens, the work of God's fingers, the moon and the stars, which God has placed there. At once we are reminded of an important fact.

GOD CREATED THEM

Right at the very beginning of the Bible we read that 'God said, "Let there be lights in the firmament of the heavens to divide the day from the night; and let them be for signs and seasons, and for days and years; and let them be for lights in the firmament of the heavens to give light on the earth"; and it was so. Then God made two great lights: the greater light to rule the day, and the lesser light to rule the night. He made the stars also' (Genesis 1:14–16). David said in another of his psalms, 'The heavens declare the glory of God; and the firmament shows his handiwork' (Psalm 19:1).

Have you ever thanked God for making the sun, the moon and the stars? We'd be in trouble without them! Have you ever realized how cleverly God has placed the stars? Many of us have enjoyed the kind of book where we can make pictures by joining up dots with straight lines. Well, God has placed the stars in the sky in groups of dots which people have been able to join together in their minds with imaginary straight lines to make shapes or patterns which we call constellations. Down through the centuries these constellations have been very useful to sailors who have been able to look up at them at night to make sure they are sailing in the right direction.

The Old Testament introduces us to some of the constellations we can see in the night sky. Amos, another shepherd, says that God 'made the Pleiades and Orion' (Amos 5:8). Job goes one further and says that God 'made the Bear, Orion, and the Pleiades' (Job 9:9). Do you know what these constellations look like? Look at the patterns below and then see if you can see them in the night sky on a clear night. This is what the Bear looks like:

Astronomers normally call it the Great Bear, but it has lots of other titles. Some people know it better as the Plough or the Big Dipper or David's Chariot. This constellation can be very useful to navigators. If we think of it as the Plough, the two stars on the right (furthest from the long handle on the left) point straight up to Polaris, the Pole Star, which is directly above earth's North Pole. So this constellation shows us exactly where North is and if we know that, we can work out all the other directions, East, West and South. Wouldn't that be useful if you got lost in the countryside and didn't have a compass with you?

The next constellation, Orion, is probably the most glorious sight in the night sky. It's more or less over the Equator and it looks something like this diagram on the next page.

Orion is supposed to represent a hunter. There are seven main stars, of which the three across the middle are called Orion's Belt. Just below them on a very clear night you can see three more faint stars going straight down and these have been described as Orion's sword hanging from his belt. If

you look closely at stars you can see that some of them give off slightly different colours. The apostle Paul wrote that 'one star differs from another star in glory' (1 Corinthians 15:41). That is certainly true of the stars that make up Orion; the top left star has a reddish tinge, while the bottom right star has a bluish tinge.

Well to the left of Orion, as seen from the northern hemisphere, there are two pairs of stars which have been described as Orion's two hunting dogs. One of the lower pair is Sirius, the Dog Star, the brightest star in the sky, apart, of course, from the sun, which is our special star. In fact six of the thirteen brightest stars in the sky can be seen in and around Orion. Now here's a mind-boggling fact—Sirius is eight light years away from the earth, or forty eight million million miles away from us! And it's actually one of the nearest stars to earth! God's universe is so big that we cannot begin to take it in. How wonderful God himself must be!

To the right of Orion, as seen from the northern hemisphere, is the other group of stars mentioned by Amos and Job, the Pleiades. Unlike the stars in the Bear and Orion, these stars are all bunched up together and are best seen through binoculars or a telescope. They have been described as 'the fairest sight in the whole panorama of the night sky.' David, Amos and Job were all able to look up at the night sky and exclaim 'What a wonderful sight! My Father in heaven created all this!' Can you say the same? God created them. He can also do something else to them.

GOD CONCEALS THEM

He commands the sun, and it does not rise; he seals off the stars (Job 9:7).

There are times when you can go outside, find a nice dark spot, look up at the sky and see nothing at all. What has gone wrong? Where have the stars gone? Job tells us that they are still there, but God can hide them behind the clouds. Some years ago a group of boys from our local Bible class went to Box Hill in Surrey to try to get a sighting of the famous Halley's Comet, but they couldn't see it. In fact they couldn't see anything at all, not even the stars or the moon, it was so cloudy. God can conceal the stars, so we are not able to stargaze just when we want! But one day God is going to do something even more drastic with the stars.

GOD WILL CHANGE THEM

The heavens are the work of your hands. They will perish, but you remain; and they will all grow old like a garment; like a cloak you will fold them up, and they will be changed. But you are the same, and your years will not fail (Hebrews 1:10–12).

Those verses are speaking about God the Son, the Lord Jesus Christ. He created the heavens and everything in them, but, unlike him, they won't last for ever. He is going to change them. The Bible says that one day there will be 'a new heaven and a new earth, for the first heaven and the first earth had passed away' (Revelation 21:1), but God will be the same as he always has been. So when you look up into the night sky and enjoy the view, never forget our glorious God who made it all and who will change it all.

Having considered the heavens, David had something else to consider.

Man's character—'When I consider ... what is man?'

What can we say about people when we compare them to God and his glory? What is man and what has man become?

MAN IS WEAK

Do you believe that? After all people can do so many things. We can send up rockets and even land on the moon. But try to think about the things people can't do. God can create something out of nothing; people can only make things when they have something to start with. We can send up satellites which can sometimes be seen in the sky, but we can't create stars or a moon! God conceals the sun, moon and stars when he wants; people only do that by accident with all the pollution that our factories, fires and cars produce. We don't seem to have any control over these things!

In past centuries, before people had all sorts of machines, instruments and computers, it could cause a very serious situation if God hid the stars from their sight. Do you remember the story about the apostle Paul when he was sailing to Rome as a prisoner? His ship sailed into a tremendous storm and Dr Luke recorded in his log of the voyage, 'Now when neither sun nor stars appeared for many days, and no small tempest beat on us, all hope that we would be saved was finally given up' (Acts 27:20). Because they couldn't see the stars, they couldn't navigate properly and had no idea where they were. They were lost! Luke continues, 'When it was day, they did not recognize the land' (Acts 27:39). It was only when they all managed to swim safely to shore from the sinking ship that they found out that they were on an island called Malta.

So you can see how weak human beings can be when God just hides the stars! One day God is going to change the heavens. People will never be able to do that. This is what God said to Job—'Can you bind the cluster of the Pleiades, or loose the belt of Orion? ... Or can you guide the Great Bear with its cubs? Do you know the ordinances of the heavens?' (Job 38:31–33). No person can change the position of the stars in the sky. Who can undo or tighten up Orion's belt? Who can take away Orion's sword or his dogs? Who can dismantle the Plough or unhook the blade from the handle? Who can scatter the stars bunched up in the Pleiades? One day God will do all of that and more, but it sounds silly even to ask whether people can do it. When we compare people to God, we have to say that man is weak. But it gets worse.

MAN IS WICKED

This can be shown in so many ways, as Agur did in our opening chapter when he seemed to be thinking of the Ten Commandments and the way in which we all break them. But here we're going to think about just one way in which mankind has been wicked. Remember that sin is when we go our own way instead of God's way. Still thinking about the night sky, this is what God commanded—'And take heed, lest you lift your eyes to heaven, and when you see the sun, the moon, and the stars, all the host of heaven, you feel driven to worship them and serve them, which the LORD your God has given to all the peoples under the whole heaven as a heritage' (Deuteronomy 4:19).

The sun, moon and stars are supposed to bring praise to God (Psalm 148:3) and people are supposed to worship God, not them. In fact God has told us not to worship anything he has created. But can you guess what so many people have done? Yes, they have become sun-worshippers, moon-worshippers and star-worshippers. And they still do that sort of thing today. Some people try to tell their fortunes or to find out what the future holds for them by looking at what it says under their star sign in newspapers and magazines. God says that astrology is useless (Isaiah 47:13–14). He hates it and tells us not to have anything to do with it. But so many people love it and can't see any harm in it. They go their way instead of God's way. It's a sin. The only proper way of looking at the stars is to see them in the night sky and to give God all the praise for his lovely creation.

'When I consider ... what is man ... that you visit him?' asked David. The time has come to complete David's question.

God's care

If you read right through Psalm 8 you'll find a strange thing. David asks this question, but never really answers it. He goes on to show how God cares for people, but he has no idea why! Why does God love us, the weak and wicked people that we are? Why? Simply because he loves us! The heavens remind us how much God cares for us, and four great events make this even clearer.

CHRISTMAS

God set a special star in the sky to announce the birth of his Son, our Saviour, the Lord Jesus Christ. The wise men followed it all the way to the manger in Bethlehem. 'When they saw the star, they rejoiced with exceedingly great joy' (Matthew 2:10). Some astronomers say that the star was Halley's Comet or a Supernova. I have no idea what it was, but the star of Bethlehem should make us rejoice as well, because God cares for us and has sent his Son to save us from our sins. But now travel from that happy scene in Bethlehem to a sad sight outside Jerusalem some thirty three years later.

CALVARY

Jesus was hanging on the cross, suffering terribly, when something awesome happened in the sky. 'Now it was about the sixth hour, and there was darkness over all the earth until the ninth hour. Then the sun was darkened' (Luke 23:44–45). The sun should have been at its highest point in the sky during this period of terrible darkness from noon to three o'clock in the afternoon. But God had hidden the sun as Jesus was separated from his loving heavenly Father while suffering the punishment for your sin and mine. This really does show how much God cares for us.

Do you remember what we discovered about man's character? Firstly, man is weak. The apostle Paul wrote that 'when we were still without strength, in due time Christ died for the ungodly' (Romans 5:6). Secondly, man is wicked, and a couple of verses later Paul continued, 'But God demonstrates his own love toward us, in that while we were still sinners, Christ died for us' (Romans 5:8).

Have you ever realized that God cares so much for you? And as if to remind the whole world of what happened on the cross at Calvary, God has placed two similar constellations in the skies, one above the southern half of the earth and the other above the northern half. Can you guess the shape? They're called the Northern Cross and the Southern Cross; the Northern Cross looks like the diagram on the page opposite.

Some amazing things happen when people look up at the sky. The Roman Emperor Constantine saw a shining cross in the sky and made Christianity the official religion. It's very unlikely that he actually became a real Christian himself, but looking up at the sky really did prove to be a great turning-point in the life of another man a long time ago.

CONVERSION

One day way back in Old Testament times, Abram, better known to us as Abraham, had the greatest experience possible. God's word came to him. God then 'brought him outside and said, "Look now toward heaven, and count the stars if you are able to number them." And he said to him, "So

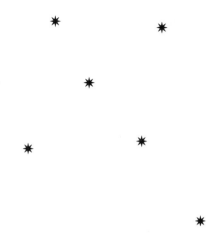

shall your descendants be." And he believed in the LORD, and he accounted it to him for righteousness' (Genesis 15:5–6).

Can you see what happened to Abram? He looked at the night sky, trusted in God who created it all and got converted! Have you had that experience? Are you willing to listen to God's Word and believe? It has been said that 'If all the stars in heaven were grains of sand, there would be enough of them to cover the whole of Britain over fifty yards deep.' That's a staggering thought. But even more amazing is that the God who made all the stars to shine cares for you so much that he sent his Son, the Lord Jesus Christ, to be crucified and to bleed to death on the cross for you. Have you thanked him and trusted him to become your Saviour? Your conversion will be the greatest event in your life! But there is one other great event we must mention in connection with the heavens.

CHRIST'S SECOND COMING

We've already hinted at what is going to happen. This is how the Lord Jesus Christ himself described the event:

The sun will be darkened, and the moon will not give its light; the stars will fall from heaven, and the powers of the heavens will be shaken. Then the sign of the Son of Man will appear in heaven, and then all the tribes of the earth will mourn, and they will see the Son of Man coming on the clouds of heaven with power and great glory (Matthew 24:29–30).

That will come as a terrible shock to all who are not trusting in the Lord Jesus Christ as their Saviour, but those who have been converted are able to look forward to the change and 'for new heavens and a new earth in which righteousness dwells' (2 Peter 3:13). Can you look forward to meeting Jesus? If so, you'll still face plenty of problems on the earth in the meantime, but whenever you do have any trouble you can cast 'all your care upon him, for he cares for you' (1 Peter 5:7).

'When I consider ... what is man ... that you visit him?'

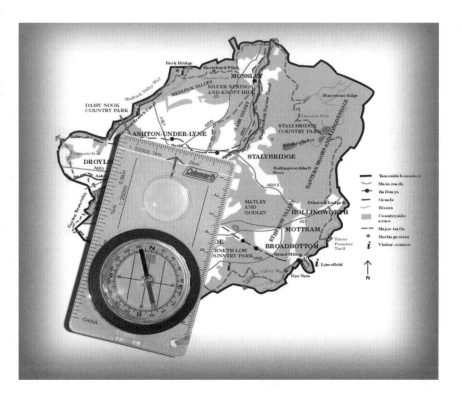

Good map-reading

D o you enjoy geography? It's a very big subject all about the earth and its peoples. Agur certainly had an interest in it and we can see something of that in some of his opening questions in Proverbs 30:4—'Who has gathered the wind in his fists? Who has bound the waters in a garment? Who has established all the ends of the earth?' Geography reminds us again of the Lord God who created everything.

My favourite part of geography has always been maps. When I first went to school at the age of five, I well remember spending most of my first day drawing London bus routes! How many different kinds of maps can you think of? They come in all shapes and sizes. The biggest ones are usually atlases, large volumes containing maps of every country in the world. Many maps are of the folded-up variety. Have you ever tried to fold one up again after opening it? That's not always an easy thing to do properly! There are country maps, county maps, city maps, railway maps, bus maps, river maps, museum plans, and you can even get a book full of maps of mazes—would you regard that as cheating?

Some parts of the Bible almost give us a picture of a map in words. The second half of the book of Joshua guides us right round the boundaries of the twelve tribes of Israel; the third chapter of Nehemiah gives us a guided tour around the walls of Jerusalem. The book of Acts almost maps out some of the apostle Paul's missionary journeys. Even the layouts of the Old Testament tabernacle and temple are virtually mapped out in words.

But the best map of all is the Bible itself, the great spiritual map of life, drawn by God the life-giver. We're going to look at the reasons for having maps and the requirements of a good map. Psalm 119, by far the longest chapter in the Bible, will teach us many important lessons about the Bible, our map of life.

The reasons for having maps

What is the point of having a map? I think a map has two main purposes— it should point the way and, to put it another way, it should prevent wandering. Its role is to help us go in the right direction and avoid going in the wrong direction. That's exactly what the Bible can do for us.

Psalm 119 starts like this—'Blessed are the undefiled in the way, who walk in the law of the LORD! ... They also do no iniquity; they walk in his ways' (vv.1,3). The psalmist is talking about people who obey God's word. The result is that they go in the right way, God's way. Later on the psalmist adds, 'I will run the course of your commandments ... And I will walk at liberty, for I seek your precepts' (vv.32,45).

But it's one thing to have a map which shows us the right way; we also have to follow what the maps says or we will end up going the wrong way! Do you remember the part of John Bunyan's *Pilgrim's Progress* where the pilgrims Christian and Hopeful are given a kind of map to get them through a particular part of their journey? As they travel on, they suddenly reach a fork in the road and instead of looking at the map, they take the advice of a stranger. However, he deliberately points them in the wrong direction and they end up getting into big trouble. We need to obey God's Word otherwise we too will end up going the wrong way and wander into trouble in our lives. The psalmist was afraid of doing that, so he prayed to God, 'Oh, let me not wander from your commandments' (v.10).

The requirements of a good map

Now that we've seen why we need maps, we need to be sure about our map of life. A good map can be a valuable friend, but a bad map can prove to be worse than useless! A map needs to pass at least five tests.

A MAP MUST BE COMPLETE

To be most useful a map needs to show as much detail as possible. Have you ever tried to use a map that doesn't show the road or the place you are trying to find? It's not much help. If you're travelling by train or bus, it helps to know where to get off, how far you've then got to walk and in which direction. Incomplete maps, such as some railway maps which don't show all the possible routes, can be a nuisance!

The word of God is as complete and detailed as it needs to be. There are secrets which God has chosen not to share with us—we don't need to know them—but in his word God has told us everything we need to know. Do you remember what Agur said about it? 'Do not add to his words' (Proverbs 30:6). We don't need to add anything. God's Word is complete and wonderful enough as it is! In Psalm 119 the psalmist prays, 'Open my eyes, that I may see wondrous things from your law … Your testimonies are wonderful' (vv.18,129).

One of the great things about the Bible is that it is full of variety. There are so many different things to read in it. Psalm 119 consists of 176 verses and nearly every one of them refers to God's Word in one way or another. If you look through it you'll find the word of God described in many different ways. It's called by all the following titles:

- God's law (v.1)—what he commands as our God and King.
- God's testimonies (v.2)—his personal witness to the truth.

- God's ways (v.3)—the ways in which he works and which we should follow.
- God's precepts (v.4)—his rules and prescriptions for a right kind of life.
- God's statutes (v.5)—the instructions he has recorded to last for ever.
- God's commandments (v.6)—the orders he had handed down for our safe keeping.
- God's judgements (v.7)—by which we are tested and should make our decisions.
- God's word (v.9)—the communication of his thoughts in speech and writing.
- God's ordinances (v.43)—the just and good standards he sets for us.

When we put all of these together, we should get some idea of how varied, detailed and complete God's Word, the Bible, really is.

A MAP MUST BE CORRECT

Accuracy is essential! It would be better not to have a map at all than to be using one with mistakes in it! On two occasions I have been approached by people hunting for a fairly new road near where I live. But they were looking for this new road a quarter of a mile away from where it is! How could they have gone so wrong? Well, the new map they were using had got the road printed in the wrong place! When a museum about the fictional detective Sherlock Holmes opened in London's Baker Street, the first bus map to include it had it printed on another road altogether. Anyone using that bus map to try to find the museum would have needed the detective skills of Sherlock Holmes himself! Maps need to be correct and can cause all kinds of problems when they contain mistakes like these.

Some people try to tell us that the Bible is full of mistakes and can't be trusted. If they are right, the Bible must be worse than useless and we are all in a great deal of trouble. But these people are the ones who have got it all wrong. Remember what Agur said—'Every word of God is pure' (Proverbs 30:5). God's Word, the Bible, is accurate, true and correct. Psalm 119 repeats this fact many times—'All Your commandments are faithful' (v.86); 'Your law is truth' (v.142); 'all Your commandments are truth' (v.151); 'The entirety of your word is truth' (v.160). I love the last of these verses in the Authorized Version where it is translated, 'Thy word is true from the beginning'—even the early chapters of Genesis, which so many people try to dismiss as myths, are completely true. God's Word, the Bible, is true and correct; and that goes for all of it!

A MAP MUST BE CONTEMPORARY

To be of much use a map must be up to date. Lots of things change and what was once correct soon becomes out of date. New roads get built, railway lines and stations close (or even open!), bus routes and numbers get altered and parts of the coastline even collapse into the sea! I remember once looking for a particular church, but when I came to the road in which it was supposed to be, I discovered that the road had gone and a housing estate had been built over it! My map was too old to show the change. It's very interesting to look at old maps, especially those which are over 100 years old, and to see how much has changed. Looking at old maps of the area in which I live reveals that the names of several roads and of a railway station have been changed, part of a railway line has since been built, and some roads, including the one in which I live, didn't even exist in those days! Imagine trying to use those maps today! We'd soon get lost!

Some people try to tell us that the Bible is out of date. They may say that it used to be correct, but things have changed in the world, and the Bible is no longer correct. Don't let them mislead you. They're not telling the truth. The writer of Psalm 119 seems to have been aware of the sort of things that so-called clever people tend to say. He tells us several times that God's Word is not only correct, but that it is correct for ever. It's contemporary, totally up to date.

This is what he tells us—'Forever, O LORD, your word is settled in heaven' (v.89); 'Your righteousness is an everlasting righteousness, and your law is truth' (v.142); 'The righteousness of your testimonies is everlasting' (v.144); 'Concerning your testimonies, I have known of old that you have founded them forever' (v.152); 'The entirety of your word is truth, and every one of your righteous judgements endures forever' (v.160). The Bible is as up to date today as when it was first written. You and I can still trust what it says.

A MAP MUST BE CLEAR

We saw earlier that a map needs to be complete and detailed, but it is possible for a map to try to show too much in a small space. It can get too cluttered and confusing. If you have used road maps, you may have discovered something very strange. So often the road or place you are looking for is on the edge of the map, or, even worse, just off the map, or it's right on a fold, or half on one page and half on another, several pages on in another part of the book! Map-reading isn't always made easy.

The Bible does contain some very difficult things, but God is not a God of confusion. The basic message of the Bible is very clear indeed. Our problem as sinners is that we are so often blind to what the Bible is saying. But the word of God is actually given to us to help us understand. Psalm 119 says some very encouraging things about God's Word—'Your word is a lamp to my feet and a light to my path' (v.105); 'The entrance of your words gives light; it gives understanding to the simple' (v.130). God's Word has not been written to get us into trouble, but to get us out of trouble!

A MAP MUST BE COMMUNICABLE

The final test of a good map is to see whether what it shows can be communicated to the map-reader. Can the people looking at it understand it for themselves? But it goes further. Good map-readers ought to be able to communicate to other people the information they have found on the map. It's good if they know the way themselves, but even better if they can then point it out to others. Many car drivers prefer to have one of their passengers acting as a navigator.

The message of the Bible is one that can be communicated. Aided by God, the good Bible-reader is one who understands the message for him or herself and who can then pass it on to others. The writer of Psalm 119 was able to do just that—'I will speak of your testimonies also before kings, and will not be ashamed' (v.46); 'Let those who fear you turn to me' (v.79). This man was in a position to help others because he himself so loved and knew God's Word.

How much do you love the Bible? Can you understand its message? In case you can't, I'd like to close this chapter by showing you the way. The Lord Jesus Christ said that there are two ways in life, a wide road that leads to destruction and a narrow path that leads to eternal life (Matthew 7:13–14). All of us begin by travelling along that wide road which is called 'my way' and by ourselves we can't do anything at all to get across to the narrow path which is called 'God's way'.

In Isaiah 53:6 we read, 'All we like sheep have gone astray; we have turned, every one, to his own way'. That means that all of us have got ourselves lost in our lives. We've all gone our own way instead of God's way. We've all sinned against God who created us and we all deserve the punishment for which we are heading on the wide road called 'my way'. But Isaiah goes on to tell us that God in his love for us has done an amazing thing—'the LORD has laid on him the iniquity of us all.' Somebody else has been punished for our sins in our place. Who could it be? It was the Lord Jesus Christ, the Son of God, who died on the cross for sinners.

Would you like to know how to get back to God? The apostle Thomas once asked Jesus how he could know the way. 'Jesus said to him, "I am the way, the truth, and the life. No one comes to the Father except through me"' (John 14:6). To get right with God you need to come to the Lord Jesus Christ—own up about your sin, ask him to forgive you and trust him to become your Saviour. Then you'll be on 'God's way' which leads to eternal life.

Which way are you on at the moment?

A grand day out

Can you think back to the beginning of Proverbs 30? Agur talked firstly about himself (vv.2–4), then about the word of God (vv.5–6). After that he prayed to God (vv.7–9); in his prayer he seemed to be remembering some of the Ten Commandments and even to be looking forward to some of the requests the Lord Jesus Christ was to teach his disciples to pray centuries later when he gave them the prayer we know as the Lord's Prayer. In this chapter we're going to go through the Lord's Prayer. To help us, we're also going to go on an imaginary day out.

Most of us like going on outings and I hope that you'll enjoy this one.

The prayer Jesus taught his disciples tells us a lot about the Christian life and our imaginary outing is going to serve as a picture to help us learn about the life of a Christian.

The centre for Tourist Information—a place for wisdom

For an outing to go well, good preparation is necessary. After all that was said in the last chapter, I hope you've remembered to bring a map! If not, never mind; I know where we can obtain one. We have to admit that we're a bit ignorant about the city we're going to visit, so we need to acquire a certain amount of wisdom or knowledge about it. All we need to know will be found at a particular centre, a Tourist Information Centre. The people who work there know the place well; they're real experts! They can tell us what there is to see and give us the opening times of all the places of interest. If we have any questions, they will probably have the answers. They can supply us with things to help us during our visit, like a mini-guide, which will contain a map of the area, or a larger guide book with a lot more detail.

The Christian also needs wisdom to live his or her life properly and it can all be found not in a place, but in a person—'Our Father in heaven' (Matthew 6:9). He is the all-wise God who knows everything. The Bible is his word, his great map and guide book for our lives. He never shuts for lunch or during the night; the Christian can always go to him in prayer. The apostle James wrote, 'If any of you lacks wisdom, let him ask of God, who gives to all liberally and without reproach, and it will be given to him' (James 1:5). A Tourist Information Centre is very useful for the visitor, but prayer is essential for the Christian.

Now we're nearly ready to start exploring, but wait just a moment, while the psalmist introduces us to our guide—'Walk about Zion, and go all around her. Count her towers; mark well her bulwarks; consider her palaces; that you may tell it to the generation following. For this is God, our God forever and ever; he will be our guide' (Psalm 48:12–14).

The cathedral—a place for worship

The first place for us to visit is the cathedral, that great building set aside centuries ago for the public worship of God. When we go inside, however, we may not be happy with everything we find. There may be things like candles for dead people or prayers to dead saints; things like that will tell us that, sadly, the people who meet in that cathedral for services don't really have a living hope in the living God. The books being sold on the bookstall will give us some idea of whether the ministers and congregation believe the Bible to be God's true word or not and whether they think it's necessary to trust in the Lord Jesus Christ alone for their salvation. I hope they do. As we go around the cathedral we cannot fail to be impressed by the beautiful architecture, all the great columns and arches, the vaulted ceilings, the towers and the stained glass windows. We can stand and look up in wonder.

How much more should we think with wonder about God and pray, 'Hallowed be your name' (Matthew 6:9)! Sometimes it's possible to get carried away with the place where we meet for services and to forget about God himself. Jesus once met a woman who started going on about places of worship. She said, 'Our fathers worshipped on this mountain, and you Jews say that in Jerusalem is the place where one ought to worship' (John 4:20). Jesus had to correct her, and declared, 'the hour is coming when you will neither on this mountain, nor in Jerusalem, worship the Father. … the true worshippers will worship the Father in spirit and truth' (John 4:21,23). Did you know that there is no temple, no cathedral, no church building in heaven? During his great vision of the heavenly city the apostle John recorded, 'I saw no temple in it, for the Lord God Almighty and the Lamb are its temple' (Revelation 21:22). God himself is worshipped perfectly in heaven and there's no need for any cathedral there! Here on earth the Christian ought to aim to live the Christian life in such a way that everything in it plays a part in worshipping God. The apostle Paul wrote, 'I beseech you therefore, brethren, by the mercies of God, that you present your bodies a living sacrifice, holy, acceptable to God, which is your reasonable service' (Romans 12:1).

You'll know that the next phrase in the Lord's Prayer says 'Your kingdom come', but we're not going to think about that now, because God's kingdom is also mentioned at the very end of the prayer and we'll talk about it then. But now that we've tasted the medieval atmosphere of cathedral choir, crypt and cloisters, it's time to get out in the open air for something completely different. We're going to go on a walk. Depending on where you are this may take several forms. It may consist of a city trail, like the London Silver Jubilee Walkway, a coastal path, a canal tow-path or a countryside walk. But we haven't got time for one of them; our walk won't take long and it will end exactly where it starts!

The city wall—a place for walking

The best place in England for a walk right round the city walls and over all the city gates has to be Chester and it's only a short distance from Chester Cathedral to the city wall. London's wall walk is nowhere near as impressive, as only bits and pieces of the old wall remain, and as long ago as the 1760s gates such as Aldgate, Bishopsgate, Moorgate, Cripplegate and Aldersgate all got demolished to make way for road traffic!

Walking is very important; in fact walking, just like worship, is another description of the Christian life, How should Christians 'walk'? The next part of the Lord's Prayer tells us—'Your will be done on earth as it is in heaven' (Matthew 6:10). Just look at that request backwards:

- 'in heaven'—that's our pattern, our example for living.
- 'on earth'—that's our place, where we are to live for God.
- 'be done'—that's our part. We're the ones to do it.
- 'your will'—that's God's purpose, what he wants done.

The way in which a Christian behaves is important. The apostle John says that those who claim to be Christians ought 'also to walk just as [Jesus] walked' (1 John 2:6). We are to follow our guide even if at times it seems a bit like a Mystery Tour and we can't see clearly where he is leading us. 'For we walk by faith, not by sight' (2 Corinthians 5:7). God has a will for us to carry out for him, as the apostle Paul wrote—'For we are his workmanship, created in Christ Jesus for good works, which God prepared beforehand that we should walk in them' (Ephesians 2:10). Christians are to 'walk as children of light ... finding out what is acceptable to the Lord' (Ephesians 5:8,10) and we need to be very careful how and where we walk (Ephesians 5:15). After all, it's not very pleasant to trip up and fall flat on your face, is it?

Well, I don't know about you, but all this walking has worked up my appetite and as it's already gone midday, it's time to have a break anyway. We need to find a nice place for lunch.

The café—a place for wants

What would you like to eat? How about plaice, chips and peas with bread and butter, followed by some ice cream and a refreshing pot of tea? That will do nicely. It's all we need; but we do have a need. We've used up energy and we have wants. We want a rest and we want a meal. It doesn't have to be anything posh and expensive, just a good plain meal that will keep us going for the afternoon until we need another meal! That's the funny thing about food. You have to keep on eating day after day.

It's the same in the Christian life. Things that happen to us in life can make us weary and hungry for God to meet our needs and so Jesus taught us to cry, 'Give us this day our daily bread' (Matthew 6:11). Actually, it's not just things that we need. Above all we need God. The request Jesus taught in a prayer is actually answered in his person! Do you remember when he fed the five thousand? Afterwards there was a great debate about bread. The people 'said to him, "Lord, give us this bread always." And Jesus said to them, "I am the bread of life. He who comes to me shall never hunger, and he who believes in me shall never thirst"' (John 6:34–35). The Christian who feeds daily upon the word of God and who seeks God daily in prayer is going the right way about getting his spiritual appetite satisfied. God has never promised to give us all the things we think we'd like to have, but he has promised to give us everything that we really need to have. Jesus said, 'seek first the kingdom of God and his righteousness, and all these things shall be added to you' (Matthew 6:33).

I hope you've enjoyed your lunch. It's time to continue on our outing. As it's lunchtime, the streets have got very busy with sightseers and shoppers and we find ourselves right in the middle of the crowd.

The crowd—a place for wandering

In fact, we're getting carried along by the crowd to our next place of interest—or are we? Where are we? We forgot to consult the map and we seem to have lost sight of our guide. We're doing the very thing that a map should stop us doing—we're wandering. We've gone the wrong way! We must stop before we go any further. But we're not hopelessly lost; we've still got our map and guide book. We could retrace our steps to the café and start again from there, or we could follow the signs back to the Tourist

Information Centre and get the staff to help us again. It can certainly make you feel very foolish when you go the wrong way, especially if you have wasted a lot of time; it's even worse if you have led others astray as well. But there's a way back.

It's exactly the same in the Christian life. The crowds of people who don't know the Lord Jesus Christ as their Saviour are going astray 'like sheep not having a shepherd' (Mark 6:34). Sometimes it's possible for the Christian to follow them instead of following God's Word and sometimes a Christian can get so led astray that he loses sight of God, the guide. But the Christian isn't hopelessly lost. He can come right back to 'our Father in heaven' and pray, 'And forgive us our sins' (Luke 11:4). The apostle John wrote down this lovely promise for those who come back to God—'If we confess our sins, he is faithful and just to forgive us our sins and to cleanse us from all unrighteousness' (1 John 1:9). The true Christian doesn't want to wander away from God, but it can and does happen; the same psalmist who prayed, 'Oh, let me not wander from your commandments!' (Psalm 119:10) had to confess at the very end of the psalm, 'I have gone astray like a lost sheep; seek your servant, for I do not forget your commandments' (Psalm 119:176). Are you a Christian who has followed the crowd and gone astray from God? Break away from the crowd and go back to the Lord Jesus Christ. He's waiting to welcome you back into the right way.

Well, after that unfortunate hiccup our outing continues with a visit to one of the most interesting and exciting places in the city, the castle, an ancient reminder of warfare.

The castle—a place for warfare

Not all castles are very exciting. Some are so ruined that there isn't much left to see, but others still stand in all their glory. At Sherborne in Dorset there are two castles, one a ruin and the other a much newer castle built by Sir Walter Raleigh. The ruin looks very picturesque, but as a castle it's totally useless. You couldn't even defend yourself against the rain, let alone against an attacking army! The newer castle is more like a stately home and it would be possible to live very comfortably in it. One of the main reasons for the existence of so many ruined castles in England is the English Civil War in the seventeenth century. Bridgnorth Castle at the northern end of the Severn Valley Steam Railway has a ruined keep which leans over even more than the famous Leaning Tower of Pisa! It's interesting, but useless. In fact castles were attacked and ruined to make them useless. Other castles faced attack but still stand in all their glory. Who can fail to be thrilled by the sight of Arundel Castle, Warwick Castle and Windsor Castle? Magnificent castles like these may still bear the scars of warfare, but they still stand victorious.

This should remind us of a very important fact of the Christian life. The Christian has to face up to spiritual enemies and Jesus told us to pray, 'And do not lead us into temptation, but deliver us from the evil one' (Matthew 6:13). Attacks on the Christian can come from three different directions— on the outside from Satan, and the society in which we live, and on the inside from self. The Christian has something like a civil war raging inside him or her! The Holy Spirit of God comes to live in us when we become Christians, but we still have sinful desires in us as well and the result is like a civil war! The apostle Paul says, 'the flesh lusts against the Spirit, and the Spirit against the flesh; and these are contrary to one another' (Galatians 5:17). Similarly, the apostle Peter wrote, 'abstain from fleshly lusts which war against the soul' (1 Peter 2:11). Paul himself was concerned that he might become a ruined Christian, useless in God's service (1 Corinthians 9:27). He actually saw this happen to one of his fellow-workers—'Demas has forsaken me, having loved this present world', he wrote sadly (2 Timothy 4:10).

But others seem so different. They face all kinds of attack from Satan, society and self. It may even be possible to see that they've been badly hurt by their experiences. But they are still standing firm and seem to be even stronger Christians than they were before. What's their secret? Well, rather than running away from God like Demas, they've run to God in their distress. 'The name of the LORD is a strong tower; the righteous run to it and are safe' (Proverbs 18:10). The apostle Paul wrote to Christians under spiritual attack, 'be strong in the Lord and in the power of his might. Put on the whole armour of God, that you may be able to stand against the wiles of the devil. ... Therefore take up the whole armour of God, that you may be able to withstand in the evil day, and having done all, to stand' (Ephesians 6:10–11,13).

The afternoon is drawing on, but we've still got time to visit one more place of interest before it closes for the night.

The court—a place for wealth

The court is a great stately home or palace, of which the most famous example in England is Hampton Court Palace beside the River Thames on the very edge of south-west London. What strikes you when you visit a stately home? I'll ask you again when we've completed our tour. First we make our way through the vast gardens with row upon row of beautiful plants and flowers. Then we go inside and admire the Great Hall with its hammer-beam roof, the Grand Staircase with its painted ceiling, the richly decorated State Apartments with their great four-poster beds and the long Picture Gallery with all its portraits and tapestries. Even the kitchens seem out of this world! Some statistics may amaze you. Knole House near Sevenoaks in Kent is almost like a smaller version of Hampton Court, but it's said to have as many courtyards as the number of days in a week, as many staircases as the number of weeks in a year and as many rooms as the number of days in a year! Having completed our tour, I'll repeat the question you've been thinking about. What strikes you about what you've just seen? My impression is one of fabulous wealth. Perhaps we feel a bit upset that some people live in such luxury when many people are homeless. 'Why don't they share what they've got?' we perhaps ask ourselves, not realizing that in one sense they have been sharing it with us as we've been going round.

But do you ever ask that question when you think about God? After all, human wealth is nothing compared to God's riches. The Lord's Prayer ends by telling us that God's 'is the kingdom and the power and the glory forever' (Matthew 6:13). Cardinal Wolsey built Hampton Court—his was the power, but it didn't last long. King Henry VIII lived at Hampton Court— his was the kingdom, but it didn't last long. But God's sovereignty (his kingdom), God's strength (his power) and God's splendour (his glory) are everlasting. They last for ever! Do you dare to think, 'Why doesn't he share it with us? Why doesn't he share it with me?' I'm going to tell you something amazing. God has shared it and he still shares it today. The Lord Jesus Christ, the eternal Son of God, is the centre of heaven's glory, but listen to what he did for you—'though he was rich, yet for your sakes he became poor, that you through his poverty might become rich' (2 Corinthians 8:9). 'He left all the glory of heaven, came to earth to die on Calvary', says the chorus. On the cross Jesus became so poor that he was even cut off from his heavenly Father. All he had left was your sin and mine, and to be punished for our sin in our place he gave up his life upon the cross. But on the third day he rose again from the dead, and can save everybody who puts their faith in him alone.

Have you done that? God is very rich. He's rich in his grace, his great kindness towards us which we don't deserve; he's rich in his glory; he's rich in his goodness. He 'gives us richly all things to enjoy' (1 Timothy 6:17). Because of what the Lord Jesus Christ has done for us we can have 'treasures in heaven' (Matthew 6:20), the forgiveness of sins and a place reserved in God's everlasting kingdom. But the apostle Paul had to ask many people, 'do you despise the riches of his goodness, forbearance, and longsuffering, not knowing that the goodness of God leads you to repentance?' (Romans 2:4). I hope that you won't be foolish like them. God offers us the greatest gift possible, but we have to thank him and accept his gift.

That's the end of our outing and our study of the Lord's Prayer. I hope you've found it interesting and helpful. We haven't had time to go back to the zoo yet, following our fleeting visit in chapter 1, and we must find time to ride on the steam railway and have a day at the cricket ground, but they will have to wait until another day.

Animal-lovers

Do you like animals? There can be no doubt that Agur did. If the first half of Proverbs 30 is mainly about different types of people, in the second half he concentrates largely on different kinds of animals. Can you remember some of the eleven species he mentions? They consist of one kind of invertebrate, four kinds of birds, one kind of reptile, three kinds of insects and two kinds of mammals. He had to be an animal-lover! Perhaps he had some pets of his own!

God is also an animal-lover. The wonderful animals he has created can teach us many things. Job puts it like this—'ask the beasts, and they will teach you; and the birds of the air, and they will tell you; or speak to the earth, and it will teach you; and the fish of the sea will explain to you' (Job 12:7–8). That's exactly what we're going to do now, as we think about God's care for his animal-creation.

God shows animals much love

Here are some verses from the Psalms to prove it: 'The LORD is gracious and full of compassion, slow to anger and great in mercy. The LORD is good to all, and his tender mercies are over all his works. … The eyes of all look expectantly to you, and you give them their food in due season. You open your hand and satisfy the desire of every living thing' (Psalm 145:8–9,15–16). 'He gives to the beast its food, and to the young ravens that cry' (Psalm 147:9). God provides for them; he's glad to be their owner. In another psalm God says, 'For every beast of the forest is mine, and the cattle on a thousand hills. I know all the birds of the mountains, and the wild beasts of the field are mine' (Psalm 50:10–11).

We can trace God's love of his animals right back to the very beginning of the Bible. He took great care when he created the different species. In fact God devoted the fifth day of creation to birds, sea monsters and all other kinds of sea creatures. Then the sixth day was taken up with the creation of livestock, wild animals and all other kinds of land animals before God created human beings. Even before he had created and blessed man, God had a special blessing for the birds and sea creatures—'And God blessed them, saying, "Be fruitful and multiply, and fill the waters in the seas, and let birds multiply on the earth"' (Genesis 1:22).

Now we all know that things soon went wrong because Adam and Eve sinned against God. Their sin had a terrible effect upon the whole of God's creation, including all the animals. Before Adam and Eve sinned, animals didn't die or get killed by one another or by man. All these things are man's fault. Things got so bad in time as people sinned more and more that God was going to wipe out life on earth altogether by drowning all the people and all the animals in a worldwide flood. But in his love God didn't want to make man extinct. He decided to save the family of one man, Noah, who trusted and obeyed him, and he instructed Noah to build a boat in which they could escape the flood.

There were only eight people in Noah's family. A small boat would have been quite big enough for them. Perhaps they could have built a lifeboat, a houseboat, a canal boat, a cruiser, a yacht or a barge. But God got Noah to build a massive ark, the size of an ocean-going liner! Why spend all that time and effort? You know the answer. God didn't want all the different kinds of animals he had created to become extinct. Some have become extinct since then, of course; I believe dinosaurs (probably baby ones) went on the ark, but they couldn't survive very long after the flood, because the world had changed so much and the new climate wasn't suitable for them any more. Man had sinned and brought sickness and death to animals, so perhaps it was only right that a man should build a big boat to rescue representatives of every kind of animal. When the flood came God cared for all who were in the ark—'God remembered Noah, and every living thing, and all the animals that were with him in the ark' (Genesis 8:1). He didn't forget about them, but cared for all the animals together.

There have been other times when God has showed his care for individual animals. A simple alphabetical lesson will help us here. 'A' is for animal.

'B' IS FOR BIRDS

How God cares for the birds! Jesus said, 'Look at the birds of the air, for they neither sow nor reap nor gather into barns; yet your heavenly Father feeds them' (Matthew 6:26). Have you ever watched sparrows feeding? They're up and down all the time, but God knows their every move. Jesus said, 'Are not two sparrows sold for a copper coin? And not one of them falls to the ground apart from your Father's will' (Matthew 10:29). He cares for them all.

Now for a spot of maths! Compare that verse with this one—'Are not five sparrows sold for two copper coins? And not one of them is forgotten before God' (Luke 12:6). How can we explain the difference in values? Just think of what it's like when you go shopping. You'll often see special offers such as 'buy two tins for the price of one' or 'buy two packets and get a third free'. The tradesmen of New Testament times also had special offers! They would sell packs of sparrows, two sparrows to a pack. But if you bought two packs, they'd give you an extra sparrow for nothing. You'd get five sparrows for the price of four. What a bargain! The tradesman placed no value on the extra sparrow, but God does. Jesus tells us that not one of them, not even the extra free sparrow, is forgotten by God. We'll learn more from this a little later.

'C' IS FOR CATTLE

There are a number of places in the Bible where God shows his care for cattle. At the time of the plagues in Egypt he gave an advance warning about the plague of hail. It went like this—'Send now and gather your livestock and all that you have in the field, for the hail shall come down on every man and every animal which is found in the field and is not brought home; and they shall die' (Exodus 9:19). Even some of Pharaoh's officials took notice and as a result their slaves and cattle were kept safe.

You'll remember the story of the prophet Jonah many years later. God was threatening the city of Nineveh with judgement. Jonah was actually looking forward to seeing it happen to them and was most upset when the people of Nineveh turned back to God and were spared. Jonah needed a telling-off now! God said to him, 'should I not pity Nineveh, that great city, in which are more than one hundred and twenty thousand persons who cannot discern between their right hand and their left—and much livestock?' (Jonah 4:11). We'd expect God to be concerned about the people, but it's lovely that he was thinking of their cattle as well. We'll learn more from the book of Jonah later.

On another occasion some armies were facing a very serious water-shortage and God gave them this message through the prophet Elisha—'You shall not see wind, nor shall you see rain; yet that valley shall be filled with water, so that you, your cattle, and your animals may drink' (2 Kings 3:17).

'D' IS FOR DONKEY

There was once a false prophet, Balaam, who was making a journey of which God disapproved. As Balaam was riding on his donkey, the Angel of the Lord kept standing in the way. Balaam couldn't see him, but his donkey could. First she turned off the road into a field and Balaam hit her. Then she squashed Balaam's foot against a wall, so he hit her again. The angel continued to stand in their way. Eventually the donkey gave up altogether and lay down on the ground. Balaam got very angry indeed and hit her again with his stick. At that point the donkey had had enough and God enabled her to give Balaam a piece of her mind! Let's eavesdrop on their conversation:

Then the LORD opened the mouth of the donkey, and she said to Balaam, 'What have I done to you, that you have struck me these three times?' And Balaam said to the donkey, 'Because you have abused me. I wish there were a sword in my hand, for now I would kill you!' So the donkey said to Balaam, 'Am I not your donkey on which you have ridden, ever since I became yours, to this day? Was I ever disposed to do this to you?' And he said, 'No' (Numbers 22:28–30).

He really got it from the horse's mouth, didn't he! It was only after God opened the mouth of a dumb animal that God opened the eyes of a prophet who was acting as if he was blind. At last Balaam saw the Angel of the Lord himself. Here's how the angel told him off—'Why have you struck your donkey these three times? Behold, I have come out to stand against you, because your way is perverse before me. The donkey saw me and turned aside from me these three times. If she had not turned aside from me, surely I would also have killed you by now, and let her live' (Numbers 22:32–33). God cared for this animal and she had something to teach Balaam.

From all of this we can see that God has a heart that cares for animals. Somebody has said that there are enough 'fear not' statements in the Bible to have a different one for every week in the year. God has even included one for animals—'Do not be afraid, you beasts of the field; for the open pastures are springing up' (Joel 2:22).

If God displays much love to animals, so should people, who are created in the image of God and who are supposed to imitate God's ways. But we so often hear of animals being cruelly treated. It used to be the case that some of the donkeys who gave rides to children on beaches were mistreated by their owners; thankfully lots of them were rescued and looked after in special sanctuaries. Much of the experimentation that is carried out on animals is very cruel. Some farming methods are not very nice. There are countries where bulls are baited and animals are driven through the streets by wild crowds. God has put people in charge of his animals, but surely he doesn't mean us to treat them like this.

God actually gave the Israelites laws about their animals. Here are some of them: 'If you meet your enemy's ox or his donkey going astray, you shall surely bring it back to him again. If you see the donkey of one who hates you lying under its burden, and you would refrain from helping it, you shall surely help him with it. … Six days you shall do your work, and on the seventh day you shall rest, that your ox and your donkey may rest, and the son of your female servant and the stranger may be refreshed' (Exodus 23:4–5,12). 'You shall not muzzle an ox while it treads out the grain' (Deuteronomy 25:4)—you may wonder why. The idea was that while the cattle were working, they shouldn't have a muzzle fitted over their mouths, because that would stop them eating. Rather, they were to be allowed to eat. They'd be much happier like that and more likely to work properly, too! Animals are not designed to be tied up and caged all the time. Free-range animals are a sign of God's blessing, says Isaiah—'Blessed are you who sow beside all waters, who send out freely the feet of the ox and the donkey' (Isaiah 32:20).

Do you show love towards animals? The way we treat animals tells other people something about our characters. Somebody once said that it's possible to tell the character of a man by looking at the way in which he treats his dog! The Bible says this—'A righteous man regards the life of his animal, but the tender mercies of the wicked are cruel' (Proverbs 12:10). 'God is love' (1 John 4:8), and it shows in the way in which he is concerned for animals. For them he has much love. But this isn't the whole story. God loves animals, but he loves people even more.

God shows people more love

In one sense this is quite a surprise. Animals haven't sinned against God, so he's had no reason to stop loving them. But we have gone against God and yet he still loves us and he loves us more than he loves animals. The old hymn says:

By him the birds are fed;
Much more to us, his children,
He gives our daily bread (Matthias Claudius, tr. by Jane Montgomery Campbell).

Jesus made this clear when he spoke about the birds—'Are not five sparrows sold for two copper coins? And not one of them is forgotten before God. But the very hairs of your head are all numbered. Do not fear therefore; you are of more value than many sparrows. ... Consider the ravens, for they neither sow nor reap, which have neither storehouse nor barn; and God feeds them. Of how much more value are you than the birds?' (Luke 12:6–7,24).

Think back to the end of the book of Jonah that we looked at earlier. Jonah was so disappointed that God had not destroyed the city of Nineveh. God had to teach him a lesson. He used not an animal, but just a plant which he caused to grow up to shade Jonah from the blazing sun. Jonah liked that! But then God made the plant die and Jonah was left very hot and very bothered! He was really angry with God about the death of the plant. Jonah cared just about a plant, but God had more important things to care about (Jonah 4:9–11). Let's compare the two viewpoints:

- Jonah cared for a plant. God cared for people, who are far more important.
- Jonah cared for one plant. God cared for 120,000 people (and that may refer only to babies who hadn't yet learned their right hand from their left).
- Jonah cared for a plant he didn't make. God cared for people he'd created.
- Jonah cared for a plant without a soul. God cared for people with eternal souls.

However much we love animals, or even plants, people are more important. Some violent people, who actually claim to love animals, are prepared to attack and even injure other people to prove it! God does love animals, but he loves people even more; so should we who are created in the image of God.

Jesus ran into problems when he healed people on the Sabbath day. The religious leaders were most upset about what he was doing and Jesus had to show them that they cared more about their animals than they did about other people. One Sabbath, Jesus was about to heal a man with a shrivelled hand. The religious leaders didn't approve. Jesus asked, 'What man is there among you who has one sheep, and if it falls into a pit on the Sabbath, will not lay hold of it and lift it out? Of how much more value then is a man than a sheep? Therefore it is lawful to do good on the Sabbath' (Matthew 12:11–12).

On another occasion, Jesus healed a woman who had been crippled for eighteen years. But again it was on the Sabbath and the synagogue ruler objected. Jesus again replied with questions—'Does not each one of you on the Sabbath loose his ox or donkey from the stall, and lead it away to water it? So ought not this woman, being a daughter of Abraham, whom Satan has bound—think of it—for eighteen years, be loosed from this bond on the Sabbath?' (Luke 13:15–16).

But people weren't very quick to learn the lesson. On yet another Sabbath, Jesus again got into trouble for healing a man and had to ask again, 'Which of you, having a donkey or an ox that has fallen into a pit, will not immediately pull him out on the Sabbath day?' (Luke 14:5).

The Lord Jesus Christ had his priorities absolutely right. He was concerned for animals, but he was far more concerned for people. Christians sometimes need to be reminded about this! Do you remember that strange verse we looked at earlier—'You shall not muzzle an ox while it treads out the grain' (Deuteronomy 25:4)? The apostle Paul quotes it on two occasions to show that people are even more important than animals. He was concerned that churches should care for their leaders and look after them. Some Christians expected their leaders to spend their time serving them and to do it all for nothing, while they themselves did jobs for which they expected to be paid! Paul wrote in 1 Corinthians 9:9–10, 'it is written in the law of Moses, "You shall not muzzle an ox while it treads out the grain." Is it oxen God is concerned about? Or does he say it altogether for our sakes?' What Paul was saying was this—if the Israelites were required to feed the animals which were working for them, then Christian churches ought to provide for the people who serve them. Cattle were not so effective when they were muzzled and church workers are not so effective when they are hindered by lack of money and lack of respect. So once again we see how God teaches us to care even more for people than we do for animals. But there is something even more important.

God should receive most love

Can God love himself? Yes, he can. Although he is one God, he is one God in three persons, Father, Son and Holy Spirit. The love between one person of the Godhead and another must be a perfect love, because 'God is love' and God is perfect. God loves animals, but animals don't have souls. God loves people, but that love isn't deserved and lots of people show that they don't want it. But if we try to think of the love that exists within the Trinity, the three persons of the Godhead, we can say that it is a love which is always deserved and always accepted. This is very hard for us to take in, but in the New Testament we get a glimpse of the love that exists between God the Father and God the Son.

When the Lord Jesus Christ was baptized, God said from heaven, 'You are my beloved Son, in whom I am well pleased' (Mark 1:11). On the Mount of Transfiguration he repeated, 'This is my beloved Son' (Mark 9:7). More than once Jesus spoke of his heavenly Father's love for him (John 3:35; 5:20) which existed even before the creation of the world (John 17:24).

And yet, despite loving his Son with a perfect love, 'God so loved the world that he gave his only begotten Son, that whoever believes in him should not perish but have everlasting life' (John 3:16). It was an act of great love when God provided an ark to save Noah, his family and the animals from the flood, but it was an act of far greater love when God provided his Son to save sinners from the punishment of their sins. It was because of that love that the Lord Jesus Christ died on the cross in the place of sinners. The apostle Paul said that he 'loved me and gave himself for me' (Galatians 2:20). Can you say the same and mean it?

O dearly, dearly has he loved,
And we must love him too,
And trust in his redeeming blood,
And try his works to do (Cecil Frances Alexander).

If God loves us so much that he sent his Son to die for us, surely we should love God in return. 'We love him because he first loved us' (1 John 4:19). Do you love him? Have you trusted the Lord Jesus Christ to save you from your sins? Animals should receive much love, people should receive more love, but God should receive most love. A man once asked Jesus what was the most important commandment. 'Jesus answered him, "The first of all the commandments is: 'Hear, O Israel, the LORD our God, the LORD is one. And you shall love the LORD your God with all your heart, with all your soul, with all your mind, and with all your strength.' This is the first commandment. And the second, like it, is this: 'You shall love your neighbour as yourself.' There is no other commandment greater than these"' (Mark 12:29–31). So we should love our friends and families (and even our enemies) very much, but we should love God most of all. Do you think people have done that to God? What responses have they given to God's love?

IGNORANCE

The ignorant response of some is even shown up by animals, such as when Balaam's ignorance was exposed by his donkey. God once spoke very sadly about his chosen people Israel—'I have nourished and brought up children, and they have rebelled against me; the ox knows its owner and the donkey its master's crib; but Israel does not know, my people do not consider' (Isaiah 1:2–3). Animals have their own ways of remembering God and sometimes they do it better than we do. God spoke again to his people Israel—'The beasts of the field will honour me, the jackals and the ostriches, because I give waters in the wilderness and rivers in the desert, to give drink to my people, my chosen. This people I have formed for myself; they shall declare my praise. But you have not called upon me, O Jacob' (Isaiah 43:20–22). Even the birds showed up the ignorance of God's people. 'Even the stork in the heavens knows her appointed times; and the turtledove, the swift, and the swallow observe the time of their coming. But my people do not know the judgement of the LORD' (Jeremiah 8:7).

Think back again to the book of Jonah and this time to the whole story. Here's a little puzzle for you. Which of the following is the odd one out: a great wind, a great fish, Jonah, a plant, a worm or a sultry east wind? Which is the odd one out and why? The answer is actually Jonah, God's prophet, because he was the only one who didn't do what God told him to do! Even when he did it later, he didn't really want to. People are far too good at ignoring God who loves us so much.

IDOLATRY

Some people respond to God's love with something else which is very wicked, idolatry. In an earlier chapter we saw that some people worship the sun, moon and stars instead of God. Some people worship animals and statues of animals instead of God. They change 'the glory of the incorruptible God into an image made like corruptible man—and birds and four-footed animals and creeping things' (Romans 1:23).

In the second of the Ten Commandments God said, 'You shall not make for yourself a carved image—any likeness of anything that is in heaven above, or that is in the earth beneath, or that is in the water under the earth; you shall not bow down to them nor serve them' (Exodus 20:4–5). But what did the Israelites do only a few days later? They made a golden calf and began to worship it! Even today some people still worship statues of animals or even living animals like cats and cattle.

Nothing should take the place of God in our lives. Anything that does take his place is an idol. Is there anything in your life that you allow to do that? The apostle Paul gave some examples when he wrote that 'men will be lovers of themselves, lovers of money ... lovers of pleasure rather than lovers of God' (2 Timothy 3:2,4). Is anything stopping you from loving God who so loved you that he sent the Lord Jesus Christ to die on the cross in your place for your sins?

When you think of the ways we humans have treated God, you might expect him to hate us. But, though he does hate our sin, he loves us and he wants us to come back to him. He'll welcome us back. This is what Jesus said about the Jews who had rejected him and who were about to have him crucified—'O Jerusalem, Jerusalem, the one who kills the prophets and stones those who are sent to her! How often I wanted to gather your children together, as a hen gathers her chicks under her wings, but you were not willing!' (Matthew 23:37).

Isn't that a lovely picture that Jesus used? The hen wants to gather and protect her little chicks. Wouldn't they be silly to run away from her? Likewise, Jesus wants to save sinners. We are even more foolish to run away from him. He's willing to save you from your sin, but are you willing to come to him to be saved?

Collecting and collectors

In the second half of Proverbs 30 we have seen that Agur was an animal-lover. We can also learn that he was a bit of a collector. In fact, he was rather good at collecting things together into groups. So he tells us about some 'things that are never satisfied' and 'never say, "Enough!"' (vv.15–16), some 'things which are too wonderful' to 'understand' (vv.18–19), some things for which 'the earth is perturbed' and 'cannot bear up' (vv.21–23), 'four things which are little on the earth, but ... exceedingly wise' (vv.24–28) and finally some 'things which are majestic in pace ... [and] stately in walk' (vv.29–31).

We'll look at a few of these in later chapters, but to stay with the first heading for now, I think Agur actually gives us a very accurate description of a collector, someone who is 'never satisfied' and who can 'never say, "Enough!"' You'll know exactly what I mean if you collect something yourself. What do you collect? If you collect stamps, which is the most popular type of collecting, that makes you a philatelist. The next most popular things to collect are coins; if you collect these, you're a numismatist. In third place comes the collecting of postcards; this is called deltiology and as I collect certain kinds of postcards, I think I must be a deltiologist! There are all kinds of other things to collect of course—books, recordings, models, dolls, cards in packets of tea, phone cards, bus tickets—you name it and somebody somewhere probably collects it!

Is God a collector? Since everything belongs to him already (Psalm 50:10–11), do you think there is anything left for him to collect? What could he ever need to collect? Actually God is passionately interested in collecting people for his heavenly kingdom. We'll learn more about that as we think about those whose hobby is collecting things.

Starting

The first step is obviously to start collecting, but I have a feeling that many collectors do this without actually meaning it. If you were to ask them when, why or how they started their collections, they probably couldn't give you an answer. Perhaps they saw something that caught their interest or something interesting was given to them and before they knew it they were collecting similar things!

It was so different with God. The Bible tells us that God chose to start collecting people for his kingdom even before he created the world. It's because God loves people that he has been collecting them (Ephesians 1:4). God had the best reason possible for starting.

Seeking

Once you've started collecting, you'll probably spend a certain amount of time, effort and money seeking. The point about being a collector is that however many items you've got, there are always many others you haven't got. In the words of Agur, a collector is 'never satisfied' and can 'never say,

"Enough!"' But it's all part of the fun of being a collector to seek out the missing items and to try to fill the gaps in the collection. Serious collectors may belong to clubs or have things sent to them through the post; they may rummage around second-hand shops or charity shops or go to collectors' fairs where there are stalls run by people who specialize in particular collectors' items.

Beware if you are a collector! It can become a very expensive hobby if you're not careful. And there is so much variety. Just to take my hobby, collecting postcards of present-day views—there are map cards, multi-view cards, cards of counties, cards of cities, seaside views, countryside views, scenes of rivers, scenes of hills, the outsides (and insides) of castles and historic houses, trains in action; the list is endless and there are plenty of other kinds of postcards which I don't collect!

God is collecting people 'out of every tribe and tongue and people and nation' (Revelation 5:9) and there are going so be so many that the apostle John in his vision realized that they would be too many for anybody to be able to count (Revelation 7:9). Just to give you a glimpse of this, I want you to think about the people of God who wrote the Bible. They lived over a period of 1,500 years; they wrote in different countries and continents—Egypt, Israel, Persia, Asia and Europe. They did different kinds of jobs. The Bible was written by kings, fishermen, shepherds, governors, a tax-collector, a doctor and a tent-maker.

Collecting people has been terribly expensive for God. People have been 'bought at a price' (1 Corinthians 6:20). Do you know how God paid to buy people back from their sin? It wasn't with money—that would never have been enough. He paid the price by sending his dear Son, the Lord Jesus Christ, to shed his blood on the cross of Calvary, and God had planned to do that as well even before he created the world (1 Peter 1:18–20). His collection of people grew rapidly on the Day of Pentecost and on the days following (Acts 2:41,47). God is still seeking people today. Has he found you yet?

Sometimes collectors can be so concerned about finding something that is missing from their collections that they seem to be more interested in the ones that they haven't got than in the thousands they have got already! God may seem to be like that, because he is so concerned for sinners who are not yet saved from their sins. To help us understand that, Jesus told a parable containing three stories in Luke 15. The first story was about a shepherd who had 100 sheep; just one of them got lost and he was so concerned about it that he left the other ninety-nine sheep, while he hunted high and low for the lost sheep. Next Jesus talked about a woman who had ten coins (possibly on a necklace); one of them fell on the ground and she was prepared to hunt for it all over the house until she found it. Finally Jesus told a longer story about a father who had two sons; his younger son left home and got into all sorts of trouble. The father was so worried about him and later so overjoyed when his boy at last came home that the older son, who had stayed at home all the time, felt left out and got very jealous. These stories should remind us how important it is for people to become Christians. If you are a Christian already, do you share God's concern for people who haven't yet trusted in the Lord Jesus Christ to save them from their sin?

Saving

Although the collector is concerned to find missing items and to fill the gaps in his collection, we mustn't get the wrong idea. He's still extremely interested in all the things he has already collected. He's saving them. Having looked for them, he's now looking after them. We collectors like to take care of our precious collections; we don't want anything to get lost or damaged.

Collectors like to keep their collections in good order. Depending on what is being collected, albums (such as stamp albums), boxes or filing cabinets can be very useful. As the collection builds up, the collector will be on the lookout for better ways in which to keep it. It's good to make improvements. When I first collected postcards I used to put them in scrapbooks, four to a page. That was fine while I didn't have very many. But as the collection grew, it became very unsatisfactory. Postcards of the same place began to get scattered throughout several different scrapbooks and, despite keeping an index, it became harder and harder to keep track of what I had and what I didn't have. My hobby was becoming less and less enjoyable. Then, one day, I saw an old dressing table in a second-hand shop and, guess what, the drawers were exactly the right size for my postcards. So

I removed them from the scrapbooks and filed them in the drawers in alphabetical order of place county by county. Since then it's been possible to see at a glance whether I already have a particular postcard or not. Of course in time the collection has outgrown even the dressing table and I have had to make further improvements by buying more filing cabinets and by using good sturdy shoeboxes!

We saw earlier how concerned God is to add extra people to his collection. But he doesn't neglect the people he has already collected. He loves them very much and wants to look after them. God doesn't want any one of them to get lost or damaged. Just before going to the cross, Jesus prayed to his heavenly Father for his disciples. This is what he asked—'Holy Father, keep through your name those whom you have given me, that they may be one as we are. While I was with them in the world, I kept them in your name' (John 17:11–12). Jesus came to 'seek and to save that which was lost' (Luke 19:10) and God is going to keep them safe. Did you know that, if you are a Christian, the Lord Jesus Christ actually speaks up on your behalf in heaven now? 'He is also able to save to the uttermost those who come to God through him, since he always lives to make intercession for them' (Hebrews 7:25).

God is always looking to improve his collection of people and to make them better and better people. Sometimes he makes changes in our lives and circumstances to achieve that goal, just as I improved my postcard collection by changing it around. God wants Christians to become more and more like the Lord Jesus Christ, to 'grow in the grace and knowledge of our Lord and Saviour Jesus Christ' (2 Peter 3:18). Some collectors are not very good at arranging their collections and everything ends up confused and in a great muddle, as was beginning to happen to my postcards. God isn't like that. He's 'not the author of confusion' (1 Corinthians 14:33) and in his church he wants everything to 'be done decently and in order' (1 Corinthians 14:40).

Did you realize that you have a part to play in that? God can keep his people, but he also wants his people to play their part to keep themselves in his love (Jude 21). God can improve his people, but he wants them to work at improving themselves. If we are Christians, God gives us the ability to do that. The apostle Peter wrote about things that every Christian ought to collect—'giving all diligence, add to your faith virtue, to virtue knowledge, to knowledge self-control, to self-control perseverance, to perseverance godliness, to godliness brotherly kindness, and to brotherly kindness love. For if these things are yours and abound, you will be neither barren nor unfruitful in the knowledge of our Lord Jesus Christ' (2 Peter 1:5–8). How are you getting on?

Swapping?

In case you're wondering, there is one thing which collectors sometimes do, but which God never does. Sometimes if a collector gets two items the same or similar, he'll arrange to swap one with another collector in return for an item he hasn't already got. You may well have done that yourself.

Jesus assures us that God never does anything of the kind. When he rescues people from the grip of Satan, the devil, and transfers them into the kingdom of his Son, the Lord Jesus Christ, God makes sure that Satan never gets them back into his collection again. Jesus said, 'My sheep hear my voice, and I know them, and they follow me. And I give them eternal life, and they shall never perish' (John 10:27–28). What a tremendous promise! When people become Christians, they receive a life which isn't temporary, but which they will have for ever, and at no point will they ever perish. As if that wasn't enough, Jesus added a further promise—'neither shall anyone snatch them out of my hand. My Father, who has given them to me, is greater than all; and no one is able to snatch them out of my Father's hand' (John 10:28–29). If you are a Christian, you belong to one 'who is able to keep you from stumbling' (Jude 24).

But a word of warning. There is a danger of looking like part of God's collection of people without ever actually being part of it. Your conversion and trust in the Lord Jesus Christ has to be genuine in the first place, otherwise it may not stand the test of time and, even if it does seem to do that, it will never be acceptable to God either now or in eternity.

Stopping

If swapping is something which collectors do, but which God never does, one day God is going to do something which collectors never like doing. He's going to stop collecting. His collection of people for his kingdom will be complete one day. Jesus said that 'this gospel of the kingdom will be preached in all the world as a witness to all the nations, and then the end will come' (Matthew 24:14). It will then be too late for anybody else to get into God's kingdom. But at the moment there is still time to get in.

The collections of some people get so big that they end up opening museums to display everything. Sometimes they have so much stuff that they can't get it all in even then! God's collection of people, as we've already seen, is going to be so large that nobody can count them, but Jesus stated that 'in [his] Father's house are many mansions' (John 14:2). There's still room for you, if you'll trust him to save you from your sin. But don't delay! 'The Lord is not slack concerning his promise, as some count slackness, but is longsuffering toward us, not willing that any should perish but that all should come to repentance. But the day of the Lord will come as a thief in the night' (2 Peter 3:9–10). After that it will be too late to be saved.

So are you part of God's collection of people? If you are, what are you doing to enlarge his collection by helping other people to become part of it? Are you praying for them? Are you taking opportunities to tell them about the Lord Jesus Christ?

Steam locomotives

S ome things, said Agur, can never be satisfied. We saw that in the last chapter. His next collection was of things too wonderful for him to understand. The first two of these, 'the way of an eagle in the air, the way of a serpent on a rock' (Proverbs 30:19), remind us of his interest in animals. But now for something completely different! The third thing he found too wonderful to understand was 'the way of a ship in the midst of the sea'.

We can easily imagine him going down to the seaside and standing on the shore where he could watch sailing ships as they passed by. There were many kinds of boats and ships in Bible times, but there weren't many other forms of transport. If you had wanted to travel overland you would either have had to walk or ride on the back of an animal, or in a chariot or wagon drawn by an animal. Actually it's only in the nineteenth and twentieth centuries that other forms of transport have appeared. Railways, bicycles, cars, buses, coaches and aeroplanes are all comparatively recent inventions.

Are you interested in any forms of transport? Agur didn't have much choice; he could be a ship-spotter but little else. I may be wrong, but I have the feeling that he might have been a bit of a train-spotter (railfan) if he had lived in our times. If so he could have wondered at 'the way of a train on the railway tracks'. Anyway, we're going to think about the type of railway engines which have always excited train-spotters—steam locomotives.

If you had gone loco-spotting in about 1960, most of the trains you would have seen would have been pulled by steam locomotives. By my calculation there were 23,906 steam locomotives operating on Great Britain's public railways in 1923. In 1948 there were 20,326. Steam locomotives were still being built right up to 1960, but after that there was a change. It had been decided to replace steam locomotives by diesel and electric trains. The number of steam locomotives went down and down, until in 1968 the last eighty-eight were taken out of service and there were none left to work on Great Britain's railway system. Where do you think all those thousands of steam locomotives went? Where are they now? What happened to them? The train-spotter finds the answer very sad indeed.

They were precondemned and scrapped

At the end of their active lives, steam engines would be towed away to scrapyards where they would be scrapped, broken up for scrap metal. Even when a steam engine was being built and was brand new, you knew that one day, when it came to the end of its working life, it was due to be scrapped. And once they had been broken up and sold off as scrap metal, there was no way back, no second chance. It's very sad to look at old railway pictures and to see engines that once worked on the railways but are no longer with us. Who can tell how the metal of a scrapped steam locomotive got scattered and re-used or where it is now?

Engines had many good qualities, but they could do nothing to save themselves from the scrapyard. Many engines had important names, such as the Great Western King class, which were named after kings of England, but that couldn't save them from being scrapped. Other engines pulled special named trains such as the Bournemouth Belle, the Cornish Riviera, the Royal Scot, the Flying Scotsman or the Golden Arrow, but hauling posh expresses didn't prevent them from being scrapped. Some engines were very powerful and could pull very heavy goods trains; others were very fast and could travel at over 100 miles per hour, like the London and North Eastern A4 class, but these got scrapped as well. Some were scrapped despite being very old, like the little 02 class tank engines which used to be on the Isle of Wight. The last types of engines to be built, including the big and strong standard 9F class, got scrapped when they were very young—some were less than ten years old! Engines could do nothing to save themselves. From the moment they were built they were already condemned, precondemned to be scrapped.

There's a verse in the Bible that sounds as if it is speaking about steam locomotives. It refers to 'those who are appointed to die' (Psalm 79:11). Actually, it's not talking about steam engines at all. It's much sadder and far more serious than that. The psalmist is talking about people being condemned to die. Why should that be the case? Well, people are condemned to die because of their sin, because they have disobeyed God and gone their own way instead of God's way. You'll remember that in the time of Noah, God used a flood to scrap nearly the whole of the human race because of their wickedness. The Bible says that people are 'condemned already' (John 3:18), precondemned because of their sin.

Do you realize that this includes you? The Bible says that 'all have sinned' (Romans 3:23) and that 'the wages of sin is death' (Romans 6:23). We're condemned already, like prisoners who have been sentenced to death for their crimes, as still happens in some countries. Think about them as they wait in the condemned cell. They're condemned already and waiting for the death sentence to be carried out. This is a horrible thing, isn't it, and we don't like to talk about it or to think about it. But God is perfect and sinless. He can't let us into heaven with all our sin. So all of us are already condemned to end up separated from God on a terrible scrapheap in that awful place called hell. And like the steam engines we were just thinking about, there is nothing we can do to save ourselves. We may be clever or look nice, try to be good or religious, or live to be very old or famous, but none of these things can help us. And for us, like a scrapped steam engine, there can never be a second chance. The Bible says, 'it is appointed for men to die once, [and] after this [is] the judgement' (Hebrews 9:27).

Perhaps you've had enough of this and don't want to read any further. But that would be a great shame. Please don't give up now. We've looked at the bad news first, but now we're going to listen to the good news! Steam locomotives were precondemned and at the end of their working lives they were scrapped, but not all of them! This should cheer us up!

Some were preserved and saved

They couldn't save themselves; they were completely helpless. Engines needed someone to pity them and buy them before they got scrapped. In fact, when engines were being towed off to the scrapyards, you could sometimes see words chalked up on them saying things like 'save me' or 'don't let me die'. Some people love steam locomotives so much that they have been prepared to pay a great price, thousands and thousands of pounds, to save a steam engine and to get it running again.

Today there are preservation societies and steam railways all over Great Britain; the Bluebell Railway in Sussex was one of the very earliest and began in 1960. Out of all the thousands of steam engines to be built, over 400 engines of well over 100 different types have been preserved and saved. Over 200 of the saved engines came in fact from one place, a scrapyard at Barry in South Wales. At one time the scrapyard owner got so busy breaking up old trucks and other things that he largely left the steam locomotives in his scrapyard alone. Starting in 1968, steam enthusiasts started to buy up the poor old engines and in 1990 the last of the 213 engines left the scrapyard for its new home. Some of these engines had been standing out in the open air for years and years. They looked terrible, all rusty and horrible. But there were people who loved and wanted them so much that they were still prepared to buy them and save them.

Our sin makes us look horrible and offensive to God. There's nothing lovely about us, nothing that can impress God. But he loves to save sinners. That verse we mentioned earlier about 'those who are appointed to die' is in fact a prayer to God which says, 'preserve those who are appointed to die' (Psalm 79:11). God loves to answer that prayer. He does preserve and save sinners. When he punished the human race with the flood 'a few, that is, eight souls, were saved' (1 Peter 3:20). Noah and his family trusted God and were saved in the ark which God provided for them. And 'God so loved the world that he gave his only begotten Son, that whoever believes in him should not perish but have everlasting life' (John 3:16). Because of his great love for sinners like you and me, God paid a tremendous price by sending his Son, the Lord Jesus Christ, into this world so that he could die on the cross for us in our place and suffer there the punishment that we deserve for our sins. He wants to save you. Have you thanked him? Have you owned up to him that you are really a rotten sinner who doesn't deserve to be saved? Some people don't like being spoken to like that. They think they are different and that they'll be all right in the end without asking the Lord Jesus Christ to become their Saviour. But they won't be.

In one of my railway books there's a photograph of a working steam engine towing four poor old withdrawn engines off to the scrapyard. What do you think happened next? The strange thing is that the four engines which were being taken to the scrapyard have all been saved, but the working engine which was taking them there later ended up getting scrapped! In the same way, sometimes the people we don't expect to get saved do get saved, and the people we do expect to get saved don't. God doesn't save people who make out that they are good enough as they are. He saves people who admit that they are sinners and who ask him to save them. Jesus said, 'I did not come to call the righteous, but sinners, to repentance' (Matthew 9:13).

Have you done anything about this? Don't just leave it and take it for granted that, just because God is saving others, he's bound to save you. I've mentioned earlier that between 1968 and 1990 over 200 steam engines were saved from Barry Scrapyard. What I didn't say is that during those years (in fact in 1972, 1973 and 1980), a few steam locomotives in the scrapyard did get scrapped. And yet they were so near to being saved. It was very alarming when they were suddenly scrapped. Trust in the Lord Jesus Christ as your Saviour before it's too late. British Rail used to have a slogan which proclaimed, 'We're getting there'. When you think about heaven, can you say that you're getting there? It's possible to buy a booklet listing all the steam locomotives that have been preserved and saved. And God keeps a list of all the people who trust in the Lord Jesus Christ. It's called 'the Lamb's Book of Life' (Revelation 21:27—see also 20:15). Is your name in it? If not, you're not on your way to heaven.

Now what? Here you'll have to use your imagination. I want you to imagine that steam engines are actually alive and have feelings! You won't find that too hard if you know any of the Rev. W. Awdry's stories about Thomas the Tank Engine and his other locomotive friends like James the Red Engine, Henry the Green Engine, Gordon the Big Engine and Edward the Blue Engine. If some of them were going to be scrapped, but then got saved from the scrapyard, cleaned up and repaired by their new owners, how do you think they would feel towards their new owners?

Their owners would be praised and served

Of course, real engines can't praise anybody, but it is true to say that they can serve their new masters on preserved railway lines. They still can't do that in their own strength, because they are lifeless until the fireman shovels in the coal and gets the fire going so that they can get moving.

As we saw earlier, over 100 different classes of steam engine have been preserved and they come in all shapes and sizes! Some were once express engines and can pull heavy passenger trains; others are tiny tank engines, which are more at home with light trains or shunting in the yard. Some engines were already famous before they were preserved, like *Mallard* which holds the record for the fastest ever speed achieved by a steam locomotive, 126 miles per hour in 1938, just as fast as the Inter City 125 diesel trains we have today. Some engines have become famous since preservation, but most preserved engines are really quite ordinary and many of them have never even had names. But the one who preserved and saved them has every right to be praised and served.

It's exactly the same with Christians. God should be praised and served by all those he has saved. Psalm 79 hints at that; at the end of the psalm, the psalmist Asaph makes three requests to God, the second of these being the prayer we have been considering—'preserve those who are appointed to die' (v.11). The psalm then ends with these words—'So we, your people and sheep of your pasture, will give you thanks forever; we will show forth your praise to all generations' (v.13). When God saves us and begins to clean up our lives, we should likewise praise and serve him. How appropriate are the words of this great hymn:

Ransomed, healed, restored, forgiven,
Who like thee his praise should sing? (Henry Francis Lyte).

Christians don't actually have any strength of their own with which they can serve God, but they can do this with the strength which he supplies to them. All over the world there are Christians from all kinds of backgrounds and with all kinds of different abilities. But every Christian can do something to God's glory. Some people are famous before they become Christians, others have become famous as Christians, but most Christians are just ordinary people like you and me. The world at large has never heard of most Christian people, but God loves every one of them and knows every one of them by name.

Has God saved you from your sin? If he has, what are you doing for him in return to show how grateful you are? The apostle Paul wrote, 'you were bought at a price; therefore glorify God in your body and in your spirit, which are God's' (1 Corinthians 6:20).

The eruption of Vesuvius

Having written about things that are never satisfied and things too wonderful to understand, Agur next groups together things for which 'the earth is perturbed' (Proverbs 30:21), things which cause the earth to tremble. I'm going to tell you the story of a tragic event which made the earth do just that, while we have a brief break from thinking about our hobbies and interests.

Less than fifty years after the Lord Jesus Christ had been crucified and raised from the dead, Mount Vesuvius erupted and the Italian towns of Pompeii and Herculaneum were buried. At times there have been exhibitions in London about Pompeii and it's been possible to look at some of the archaeological remains. Some of you may have even been on holiday in Italy and have been able to visit the ruined towns.

We know exactly what happened because there is an eyewitness account of the disaster written in Latin by one of the survivors, the Roman author Pliny, who described the events as he saw them in two letters to the historian Tacitus. Pliny was only about eighteen years old at the time and was living with his uncle, known to us as the Elder Pliny, at Misenum, several miles across the Bay of Naples from Pompeii. As you can see from the map below, Misenum was very near Puteoli, where less than twenty years earlier the apostle Paul had arrived as a prisoner on his way to be tried at Rome (Acts 28:13).

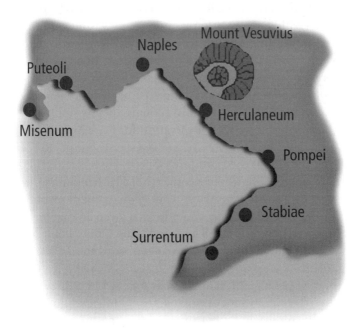

The first of Pliny's two letters is mostly about his uncle.

The Elder Pliny
It was about one o'clock in the afternoon on 24th August A.D.79. Young

Pliny's mother noticed an unusual cloud rising in the sky and brought it to the attention of the Elder Pliny, who then climbed a hill from where he could see that the cloud was coming up from Mount Vesuvius. Pliny's uncle was a very clever and scholarly man. He was very interested in nature and wrote a Natural History in thirty-seven books, which can still be read today. It's hardly surprising, then, that he had a yacht prepared so that he could go and get a closer look. Before leaving he asked his nephew whether he would like to come as well, but Pliny replied that he had some homework to finish.

Pliny's account (as translated by the late Claude Neath, one of my former Latin teachers) continues as follows—'As my uncle was leaving the house, he received a letter from Rectina, who was terrified by the imminent danger (for her villa lay just below us and there was no escape except by ship); she earnestly begged him to rescue her from such deadly peril.' Pliny's uncle was actually in charge of the fleet at Misenum and was the only person in a position to rescue this lady Rectina. She was unable to reach safety by herself and was in danger of perishing. Her only hope of salvation was that the Elder Pliny would come to her by ship.

What a picture of God's way of salvation for perishing sinners like you and me! We can't do anything to save ourselves; only one person can save us from our sins and that is the Lord Jesus Christ. He himself said, 'I am the way, the truth, and the life. No one comes to the Father except through me' (John 14:6). The apostle Peter later said, 'Nor is there salvation in any other, for there is no other name under heaven given among men by which we must be saved' (Acts 4:12). The Lord Jesus Christ could have safely stayed in heaven, but he came to this planet instead to save and rescue the perishing.

Similarly, it would have been much safer for the Elder Pliny to remain at home or to observe Mount Vesuvius from outside the danger area. However, having received a letter from poor Rectina,

He changed his first plan. He had some galleys launched and went on board himself with the intention of assisting not only Rectina but many others. He steered a direct course to the point of danger, free from fear ... By now cinders were falling upon the ships, now also pumice-stones and blackened and scorched rocks. After hesitating a little while he said to the helmsman, 'Fortune favours the brave; take me to Pomponianus.'

His friend Pomponianus was at Stabiae, just a few miles from Pompeii, and was ready to flee if necessary. So the Elder Pliny had decided to go right into the place of greatest danger in order to save others. This again reminds us of the Lord Jesus Christ—'Now it came to pass, when the time had come for him to be received up, that he steadfastly set his face to go to Jerusalem' (Luke 9:51).

Pliny's account goes on to tell us how his uncle reached Pomponianus at Stabiae and continues—

My uncle comforted and encouraged his alarmed friend and in order to soothe the other's fear by his lack of concern, he desired to be conducted to a bathroom; having bathed, he sat down and dined with great cheerfulness or with every appearance of it. Then he retired to rest and slept in what was certainly a very genuine sleep … But the courtyard's level was now rising under its cover of a mixture of pumice-stones and ashes, so much so that if he had continued longer in his bedroom, exit would have been impossible. On being aroused he returned to Pomponianus and the others. They consulted together.

Here again the Elder Pliny reminds us of the Lord Jesus Christ. There was a time when he also was fast asleep in the middle of danger when a storm blew up on the Sea of Galilee where he was in a boat with his disciples. They were terrified, but he was calm. When they woke him up, he asked them, 'Where is your faith?' (Luke 8:25). Before we go on with our story, I want you to answer that question for yourself. Where is your faith? Is it in yourself or in fortune, like the Elder Pliny's was, or is it in the Lord Jesus Christ, where it needs to be?

We must return to the Elder Pliny. By this stage, he and the others were unable to escape by sea. They sat down on the shore. The account continues—'Then the flames and the smell of sulphur scattered the others in flight; him (the Elder Pliny) they merely aroused. Leaning on two young slaves he got up but instantly fell down … When day dawned his body was found whole and uninjured—it was more like that of a sleeping man than that of a dead one.' What a sad ending. When danger was at last upon them, all of the Elder Pliny's friends ran away and left him to his death.

Likewise, when the Lord Jesus Christ was arrested in the Garden of Gethsemane, 'all the disciples forsook him and fled' (Matthew 26:56). The Elder Pliny came to save others, but it led to his own death instead. What a great sacrifice! But the Lord Jesus Christ made a far greater sacrifice. He came that we might have life and to give us life he laid down his life for us (John 10:10–11). He 'became obedient to the point of death, even the death of the cross' (Philippians 2:8). Unlike the Elder Pliny, Jesus rose again from the dead. He's alive for ever and can give us eternal life. Do you know how to receive his gift of eternal life? Read the answer yet again in John 3:16—'For God so loved the world that he gave his only begotten Son, that whoever believes in him should not perish but have everlasting life.'

The Elder Pliny wasn't a Christian. He believed that 'fortune favours the brave', but that didn't do him any good. The Bible makes it clear that God favours faith. When the Bible talks about God's grace, it means his free undeserved favour which he shows to those who put their faith in the Lord Jesus Christ alone to save them from their sins. Have you done that?

The second letter about the eruption of Vesuvius concerns Pliny himself.

The Younger Pliny

The Elder Pliny had left his young nephew at Misenum reading and studying. How like his scholarly uncle. Like uncle, like nephew! There had been earthquakes for several days, 'but that night it became so violent that the world was not only being shaken but turned upside down.' Pliny's mother came to his room. But he, just like his uncle, cared for others and had already got up in his concern for his mother. His account continues:

We sat down in the courtyard. I called for a volume of the historian Livy, and, as if nothing were the matter, I read it … Lo and behold in comes a friend of my uncle … When he saw my mother and me seated and me actually reading, he censured her patience and my indifference … No less engrossed I went on intently with my book. It was now 6 o'clock in the morning; now the buildings were tottering and there was a serious and obvious risk of the house falling down. Then at last it seemed best to leave the town.

Once again we can see that Pliny was just like his uncle. He also remained calm in the midst of great danger. In many ways he seems to have copied his uncle's lifestyle and indeed he was to become a famous writer, just like his uncle. As he and his mother left their house the ground was heaving up and down; sea creatures were being thrown up on the shore. There was a terrible black cloud and flashes everywhere. The friend who was with them ran away. As ashes fell upon them people were crying and shouting; many were praying for death. They thought it was the end of the world. It wasn't, of course; we know that. But 'the day of the Lord will come' (2 Peter 3:10) and the scene then will be even more terrifying for those who have refused to accept the Lord Jesus Christ as their Saviour. The Bible says that they will call 'to the mountains and rocks, "Fall on us and hide us from the face of him who sits on the throne and from the wrath of the Lamb! For the great day of his wrath has come, and who is able to stand?"' (Revelation 6:16–17).

In the end, darkness was replaced by light and even some sunshine. Pliny returned to Misenum with his mother; there they spent the following night wavering between hope and fear, but for them the danger was past. At this point Pliny's account comes to an end. In the disaster some perished and some were saved. It will be just the same when the Lord Jesus Christ comes again. Those who do not obey the gospel will perish, while those who have put their faith in the Lord Jesus Christ will be saved. In which group are you?

If you are a Christian, there is another lesson to learn from Pliny's account of the eruption of Vesuvius. We've seen that in many ways Pliny had copied his uncle's life and behaviour. In some ways we've seen in his uncle a faint picture of the Lord Jesus Christ. Just as Pliny copied his uncle, the Bible teaches Christians to imitate the Lord Jesus Christ:

SERVICE

In the way in which he served, Jesus set us an example. Shortly before his death he performed an act of humble service for his disciples and said, 'I have given you an example, that you should do as I have done to you' (John 13:15).

SUFFERING

In the way in which he suffered, Jesus set us another example. The apostle

Peter wrote, 'Christ also suffered for us, leaving us an example, that you should follow his steps: who ... when he was reviled, did not revile in return; when he suffered, he did not threaten, but committed himself to him who judges righteously' (1 Peter 2:21,23).

Christians should seek as far as possible to behave like the Lord Jesus Christ. He, of course, lived a perfect life and, as we are all sinners, we're not going to be able to copy him perfectly. But there are other people in the Bible who, despite being sinners like us, lived in a way which was pleasing to God; they are also examples for us to follow.

THE PROPHETS

The Old Testament prophets were good examples—the apostle James writes, 'My brethren, take the prophets, who spoke in the name of the Lord, as an example of suffering and patience. ... You have heard of the perseverance of Job... Elijah was a man with a nature like ours' (James 5:10–11,17).

PAUL

Another godly man who set some good examples in the New Testament was the apostle Paul. Read some of the things he wrote to various churches—'I urge you, imitate me. ... Imitate me, just as I also imitate Christ' (1 Corinthians 4:16; 11:1). 'Brethren, join in following my example, and note those who so walk, as you have us for a pattern' (Philippians 3:17). 'For you yourselves know how you ought to follow us, for we were not disorderly among you; nor did we eat anyone's bread free of charge, but worked with labour and toil night and day, that we might not be a burden to any of you, not because we do not have authority, but to make ourselves an example of how you should follow us' (2 Thessalonians 3:7–9).

You may still find it hard to try to follow the example of people in the Bible. They lived such a long time ago and you have never met them! You may find it easier to copy some godly Christian people you do know, perhaps relatives, friends or other people at church. If they're seeking to imitate the Lord Jesus Christ and to live in a way that pleases God, they won't be perfect, but in their lives you should be able to find things to imitate. What about those who teach the Bible to you? The Bible says,

'Remember those who rule over you, who have spoken the word of God to you, whose faith follow, considering the outcome of their conduct' (Hebrews 13:7).

Can you guess what happens next, when Christians copy those who are imitating the Lord Jesus Christ? They themselves become good examples for others to imitate! The apostle Paul was so pleased with one church which was doing this. To them he wrote, 'you became followers of us and of the Lord, having received the word in much affliction, with joy of the Holy Spirit, so that you became examples to all in Macedonia and Achaia who believe' (1 Thessalonians 1:6–7).

Are you setting a good example for others to follow? Paul told one of his fellow-workers to be in all things 'a pattern of good works' (Titus 2:7). In what respects do you think a Christian can set a good example to others? Paul listed some of them when writing to a young pastor—'Let no one despise your youth, but be an example to the believers in word, in conduct, in love, in spirit, in faith, in purity' (1 Timothy 4:12).

Pliny, though only a young man himself, became a good example to others by imitating the good example set for him by his uncle. But a word of warning here. Pliny wasn't a Christian; indeed another of his letters shows that he couldn't understand the Christian faith at all. Trying to copy good examples has never got anybody into heaven. Many people think that all they have to do to get to heaven is to try to copy the Lord Jesus Christ. They don't seem to realize that it's not even possible for them to copy him. We can't start to do that until we have first trusted in his death on the cross to take away our sin and to bring us salvation and forgiveness. It's essential to get this in the right order:

O dearly, dearly has he loved,
And we must love him too,
And trust in his redeeming blood,
And try his works to do (Cecil Frances Alexander).

Here comes the bride!

Have you been to a wedding lately? It's a happy occasion when a couple get married. But sadly, not all marriages turn out to be happy ones. Agur refers to a wedding in Proverbs 30:23, but it didn't result in a happy marriage; rather, he describes it as one of those things which makes the earth tremble, and that's no recipe for a happy marriage. If you'd like to read what God really intends marriage to be like, all you have to do is to turn to the next and last chapter of Proverbs (31:10–31) where there is a lovely description of a good wife and a really happy marriage.

The Bible actually uses marriage as a picture of the relationship between the Lord Jesus Christ and his church. In the Old Testament one of the prophecies about God's people includes these words—'as the bridegroom rejoices over the bride, so shall your God rejoice over you' (Isaiah 62:5).

Similarly, in the New Testament the Christian church is described as 'the bride, the Lamb's wife' (Revelation 21:9). One day—nobody knows when—there is going to be a great occasion in heaven. In his vision, recorded in the book of Revelation, the apostle John heard a loud chorus of voices shouting, 'Alleluia! For the Lord God Omnipotent reigns! Let us be glad and rejoice and give him glory, for the marriage of the Lamb has come, and his wife has made herself ready' (Revelation 19:6–7). Then an angel said to John, 'Blessed are those who are called to the marriage supper of the Lamb!' (v.9).

On her wedding day, the bride spends a lot of time getting herself ready, so that she looks at her very best in her wedding dress. But before the wedding day, the couple who are going to get married have a lot of things to do to get ready for their married life. That's one reason why it's usual for people to get engaged to each other some time before they are married. The Christian, who one day is going to be part of the bride of Christ in heaven, also has first a time of being engaged to Christ on earth. That time of engagement begins as soon as someone is converted and becomes a Christian.

How grateful the Christian should be to those who point the way to the Lord Jesus Christ! John the Baptist did that. He saw himself as 'the friend of the bridegroom', whose job it was to introduce people to the Lord Jesus Christ (John 3:29). The apostle Paul was another who performed this duty; he wrote to one church, 'I have betrothed you to one husband, that I may present you as a chaste virgin to Christ. But I fear, lest somehow, as the serpent deceived Eve by his craftiness, so your minds may be corrupted from the simplicity that is in Christ' (2 Corinthians 11:2–3). Paul had introduced the Lord Jesus Christ to the Corinthians and the Corinthians to Christ. Many had become Christians; they were engaged to Christ. But engagements can go wrong and Paul was worried that the Corinthians were having second thoughts and that they would not remain faithful to the one to whom they would be getting married in heaven.

Sometimes engagements can go so wrong that they get broken off and the people who were engaged to get married don't actually get married in the end. But the Lord Jesus Christ has promised never to break off the engagement with any of his people. This is what he promised—'I give them eternal life, and they shall never perish; neither shall anyone snatch them out of my hand' (John 10:28). The Christian life on earth is a time for getting to know the Lord Jesus Christ, a time for walking with Christ and for talking with Christ. This period of engagement may not always go smoothly, but for every properly converted Christian it will lead in the end to 'the marriage supper of the Lamb' and to being married to the Lord Jesus Christ for ever and ever in glory. Are you a Christian? Are you engaged to Christ? Are you going to be part of his bride in heaven?

Jesus once told a story about a wedding banquet (Matthew 22:1–14) and we're going to follow the events as they unfolded.

Reception

The kingdom of heaven is like a certain king who arranged a marriage for his son (v.2).

The story is going to be a picture about the King of Heaven, God the Father, holding a wedding banquet for his Son, the Lord Jesus Christ. It's all about 'the marriage supper of the Lamb'. Later we'll see what happened at the reception, but for the moment we must think about the preparations. A lot has to take place before a wedding and a reception. Among other things someone (these days normally the father of the bride) has to draw up a guest list and has to take the trouble to send out invitations to all the people whom the happy couple and their families want at their wedding. In Jesus' story the father of the bridegroom sent out the invitations.

Requests

[He] sent out his servants to call those who were invited to the wedding; and they were not willing to come (v.3).

It was now time for the wedding banquet and it's clear that the invitations had been sent out in plenty of time, well in advance of the great day. But the people who had been invited didn't want to come! God the Father has been sending out invitations to the wedding supper of his Son, the Lord Jesus Christ, for nearly 2,000 years. He's given people plenty of time to reply. Have you done anything about it? Will you be ready when he calls you to come? It's a great privilege to be invited—'Blessed are those who are called to the marriage supper of the Lamb!' (Revelation 19:9)—and, as we've already seen, we're invited not just to be God's guests, onlookers at the wedding, but actually to be part of the bride of Christ! And yet so many refuse God's invitation. I hope that isn't true of you.

Readiness

Again, he sent out other servants, saying, 'Tell those who are invited, "See, I have prepared my dinner; my oxen and fatted cattle are killed, and all things are ready. Come to the wedding"'(v.4).

In his further attempts to get his intended guests to come, the king emphasised that everything was ready. One of the things that takes a lot of preparation before a wedding reception is the catering. If a lot of guests are going to be invited, a lot of food has to be bought and prepared for them to eat. But the king had seen to all the catering. Nobody needed to bring any food; they simply had to come and enjoy themselves! Actually the king had gone to a lot of trouble. No cost had been spared; great sacrifices had been made.

God the Father has already provided all the catering for the wedding banquet of his Son, the Lord Jesus Christ. No animals have been sacrificed, but to make people ready to be part of the bride of Christ, it was necessary for the Lamb of God, the Bridegroom himself, the Lord Jesus Christ, to be sacrificed on the cross of Calvary. 'Christ also loved the church and gave himself for her, that he might sanctify and cleanse her' (Ephesians 5:25–26). On the cross he called out in triumph, 'It is finished!' (John 19:30), to proclaim that all had been done and that everything was ready.

On the cross Jesus worked terribly hard to win the church as his future bride. All the catering for his wedding banquet has been completed. God has catered for you to be part of Christ's bride. You don't have to bring any extras with you; you just have to come to him as you are. A well-known hymn puts it like this:

Just as I am, without one plea
But that thy blood was shed for me,
And that thou bidd'st me come to thee,
O Lamb of God, I come (Charlotte Elliott).

When invitations are sent out, they usually have the letters R.S.V.P. on them. As you probably know, these are an abbreviation of a French phrase meaning 'Please reply'. If you get an invitation which says R.S.V.P., you're expected to send an answer to the person who sent you the invitation! God expects us to answer his invitation to the wedding banquet of his Son. What reply have you given him?

Replies

But they made light of it and went their ways, one to his own farm, another to his business. And the rest seized his servants, treated them spitefully, and killed them (vv. 5–6).

Well, how do you like that? How rude and ungrateful can you get? It's very bad and an awful nuisance when people are invited to be guests at a wedding reception, but can't be bothered to send a reply. These people just ignored the king's wedding invitations and some of them even attacked the postmen for bringing the invitations to them! How have you replied to God's invitation to come to the Lord Jesus Christ? Have you just ignored it, or have you made excuses for not coming?

On another occasion Jesus told a similar story about people being invited to a banquet—'But they all with one accord began to make excuses. The first said to him. "I have bought a piece of ground, and I must go and see it. I ask you to have me excused." And another said, "I have bought five yoke of oxen, and I am going to test them. I ask you to have me excused." Still another said, "I have married a wife, and therefore I cannot come"' (Luke 14:18–20). Weren't their excuses pathetic? But any excuses which people make for not trusting in the Lord Jesus Christ as their Saviour are just as bad.

When someone is preparing a wedding reception, they have to be prepared for some upsets. Some people never bother to reply to the invitations, which is very annoying. Other people genuinely cannot come and some perhaps don't want to come; that can be very disappointing. How do you think God feels when people ignore his invitations or just make excuses for not coming to the Lord Jesus Christ? It's a far more serious matter altogether, as we shall now see.

Repercussions

But when the king heard about it, he was furious. And he sent out his armies, destroyed those murderers, and burned up their city (v.7).

Do you think he overreacted? Or did those people get what they deserved? After all, in return for his kind invitation, they had ignored him and some had even attacked and killed some of his servants. People have done exactly the same with God's invitation. So many have ignored it and, if you look through Christian history, you will see that some have attacked and killed those who have brought God's word to them. God has every right to be angry and to threaten us with eternal punishment.

But God isn't a bully; he's a God of love. When he warns us about that terrible place called hell where sinners are punished for their sins, it's not because God hates us and wants to frighten us, but because he loves us and wants to save us. To be invited to his wedding banquet is a great blessing if we accept the invitation, but it's a terrible and dangerous thing to turn it down.

So far things don't seem to have been going to plan, do they? The king had a wedding reception already, but there weren't any guests on the horizon! What could he do? He decided to go back to square one.

Repetition

First he spoke again about his state of readiness—'Then he said to his servants, "The wedding is ready, but those who were invited were not worthy"' (v.8). But he had a remedy for his problem. Anybody who is arranging a wedding reception will have a reserve list of people to invite if those originally invited can't or won't come.

So he sent out further requests or invitations—'Therefore go into the highways, and as many as you find, invite to the wedding' (v.9). Anyone and everyone is invited to God's wedding banquet in heaven.

This time there were plenty of grateful replies—'So those servants went out into the highways and gathered together all whom they found, both bad and good. And the wedding hall was filled with guests' (v.10). So in the end the reception was very well attended. It will be impossible to count the number of people who are going to be part of God's wedding banquet in heaven. The big thing for you is to make absolutely sure that you are going to be there yourself.

This could have been the end of the story Jesus told, but as is so often the case with his parables, there is a further incident which is very strange indeed. It should help us to examine ourselves and make sure that we really are on our way to heaven.

Raiment

But when the king came in to see the guests, he saw a man there who did not have on a wedding garment. So he said to him, 'Friend, how did you come in here without a wedding garment?' And he was speechless. Then the king said to the servants, 'Bind him hand and foot, take him away, and cast him into outer darkness; there will be weeping and gnashing of teeth.' For many are called, but few are chosen (vv.11–14).

This man seems to have heard the invitation and answered it. So why should he be thrown out? The reason given is that he wasn't properly dressed for the wedding. People usually wear special clothes at a wedding, not any old clothes! A wedding is not the only place where special clothes are expected. There are shops where you'll be asked to leave if the owners think you are not dressed in an acceptable way! Some restaurants won't even let a man in if he's not wearing a tie! And many people are going to be kept away from the great wedding banquet in heaven because they're not properly dressed for the occasion. It's very important to understand this properly. This has got nothing to do with the actual clothes you wear on your body or even with the clothes people wear when they go to church. Some questions will help us see what it does mean.

Do you claim to have come to Jesus? If you say that you have, consider another question. How have you come to Jesus? This man was asked, 'how did you come in here?' It's possible to think that you have come to Jesus when you haven't. Lots of people think that their good deeds bring them to Jesus. They believe that they can come to Jesus all dressed up in their good deeds. But the Bible says that even the good things we do 'are like filthy rags' in God's sight (Isaiah 64:6). It's futile trying to come to Jesus pretending that we're good, when God knows full well that we're all sinners. Our good deeds are like filthy rags and they're useless as wedding clothes for heaven.

We all need a change of clothing. Our sins have to be covered up and they can only be covered up by the perfect goodness of the Lord Jesus Christ himself. When Jesus died on the cross, he provided not only the catering for his wedding banquet, but also all the clean wedding clothes for his guests. Those who have accepted the Lord Jesus Christ as their Saviour can speak like this—'I will greatly rejoice in the LORD, my soul shall be joyful in my God; for he has clothed me with the garments of salvation, he has covered me with the robe of righteousness, as a bridegroom decks himself with ornaments, and as a bride adorns herself with her jewels' (Isaiah 61:10).

On the cross of Calvary a great swap took place. The Lord Jesus Christ, as it were, put on the filthy rags of our sin and was punished for it. In return he offers us, as it were, the lovely clean robe of his perfect goodness. Wearing that, we can get into heaven. We get changed out of our rags and into his robe only when we trust in him to be our Saviour and to take away our sin. Have you got changed yet or are you still trying to gatecrash heaven, like people who try to force their way into parties despite not having been invited? We have to come to Jesus in the right way, his way; trying to come to him in your own way is still sin. Jesus said, 'he who does not enter the sheepfold by the door, but climbs up some other way, the same is a thief and a robber' (John 10:1).

In the first part of John Bunyan's famous book *The Pilgrim's Progress*, Christian came through the gate, but he later met two other men who got onto the road by climbing over the wall. Going all the way to the gate was far too much trouble for them. They preferred to take a short cut. As far as they were concerned they were heading in the right direction for the Celestial City, so surely it didn't matter how they got there. Christian had this to tell them—'You came in by yourselves without the Lord's direction, and you shall go out by yourselves without his mercy.' Christian had been given some important things when he went through the gate—a scroll, a mark on his forehead and, of particular interest to us, the Lord's coat for him to wear instead of his own old rags. Christian reached heaven; the other two got nowhere near it.

We can get to heaven only if we come in God's way, the way God has commanded us, by owning up about our sins and by trusting in the crucified Lord Jesus Christ to save us from them. Have you done that? If not, you're not yet properly dressed for 'the marriage supper of the Lamb'. But you are invited. God wants you to come and your Christian friends want you to come—'And the Spirit and the bride say, "Come!" And let him who hears say, "Come!" And let him who thirsts come. Whoever desires, let him take the water of life freely' (Revelation 22:17).

'All things are ready. Come to the wedding' (Matthew 22:4).

We're going to the zoo!

I've been promising you another trip to the zoo. On our first visit we were in such a hurry that we didn't really have time to stop and look at the animals properly. But we'll make up for it this time as we look at Agur's fourth collection of things that interested him. You'll remember that he first spoke about things that cannot be satisfied; then he listed things that were too wonderful for him to understand; thirdly came some things which make the earth tremble. Agur's fourth group (Proverbs 30:24–28) is the most detailed of them all and this is how he introduces it—'There are four things which are little on the earth, but they are exceedingly wise' (v.24). On this visit to the zoo we're going to limit ourselves to these four creatures which are small, but wise. The great lessons they have to teach us are out of all proportion to their tiny size! We're going to be spending most of our time today in the Insect House.

Provision

The ants are a people not strong, yet they prepare their food in the summer (v.25).

You may wonder why we've gone to the zoo to look at some ants when you could have probably seen them in your garden. The reason is that these ants are a special variety which are common in Bible lands. Here they are in this enclosure marked Harvester or Agricultural Ants. They're just as tiny as the ants you can see in the garden, but very wise. During the summer months they collect seeds and store them in little galleries under the ground. By doing this they make provision for the winter, so that there will be enough food to see them through the winter months.

In an earlier chapter of Proverbs, Solomon spells out exactly what the ants have to teach us—'Go to the ant, you sluggard! Consider her ways and be wise, which, having no captain, overseer or ruler, provides her supplies in the summer, and gathers her food in the harvest. How long will you slumber, O sluggard? When will you rise from your sleep? A little sleep, a little slumber, a little folding of the hands to sleep—so shall your poverty come on you like a prowler, and your need like an armed man' (Proverbs 6:6–11).

Do you know what a sluggard is? The word 'sluggard' is connected to the word 'slug', another creature found in the garden, but so unlike the ant. While the ants can be seen bustling about, the slug crawls along so slowly that it takes ages to get anywhere or to do anything. Sluggards are lazy people who don't get things done; they let things go and fail to get ready for the future. The busy ants teach people like that to get up and to get moving before they get a nasty shock. Being lazy is connected to being wicked (Matthew 25:26) and the Bible tells us not to be 'sluggish' (Hebrews 6:12).

Which are you like, the ant or the slug? Ants make provision for the winter so that they won't get caught out by a shortage of food. The Bible tells us to make provision for eternity so that we'll be ready and not get caught out. The Lord Jesus Christ said, 'Do not lay up for yourselves treasures on earth, where moth and rust destroy and where thieves break in and steal; but lay up for yourselves treasures in heaven, where neither moth nor rust destroys and where thieves do not break in and steal' (Matthew 6:19–20). We have to get ready to meet God in eternity—'prepare to meet your God' (Amos 4:12). But how can we do that? After all, God is holy, while we're sinners who have disobeyed him and broken his laws. How can we get right with him? To find out we'll have to leave the Insect House for a while and make our way across to the Small Mammal House to find our second small creature.

Protection

The rock badgers are a feeble folk, yet they make their homes in the crags (v.26).

When we look at the label on their enclosure, we learn that rock badgers are also known as coneys or hyraxes. They're nothing like the badger as we know it. In fact, they're closely related to the elephant, hippopotamus and rhinoceros, but they're nowhere near as big or as strong as their better-known relatives. They're no bigger than rabbits! If you look into their enclosure you'll observe that they don't burrow into the earth as rabbits do, but they run in and out of the rocks among which they live. Their name in Hebrew means 'the hider'. Being so small, rock badgers are at risk of being attacked by larger animals, but they're wise. By living in holes in the rocks they find protection from their enemies—'the cliffs are a refuge for the rock badgers' (Psalm 104:18).

We all need protection from our enemies. Where can we be safe? Where can we find protection from Satan, from the society around us, and even from our own selves? All of these lead us into sin. And where can we find protection from all the sins we have committed against God? Where can we hide from God's anger on the day of judgement? The psalmist gives us the answer more than once—'God is our refuge and strength, a very present help in trouble' (Psalm 46:1); 'In God is my salvation and my glory; the rock of my strength, and my refuge, is in God' (Psalm 62:7); 'the LORD has been my defence, and my God the rock of my refuge' (Psalm 94:22).

In the New Testament, the Lord Jesus Christ is described as 'that spiritual Rock' (1 Corinthians 10:4). Just as the rock badgers find protection in the rocks, so we can find protection only in Christ, the rock of our salvation. He died on the cross of Calvary in our place and for our sins. When we put our trust in him to become our Saviour, it's like hiding in a great rock where we will be protected from our very worst enemies, including our sins and the punishment we deserve for committing them. Are you hiding in the Lord Jesus Christ or are you still exposed to great danger? Now it's time to return to the Insect House for a further lesson.

Procession
The locusts have no king, yet they all advance in ranks (v.27).

What do locusts actually look like? As we peer into their enclosure, I think we could describe them as big grasshoppers, but they're still quite small. Locusts are very wise and clever. Unlike the ants in their enclosure, who have a queen ant, and unlike bees, who have a queen bee, locusts never have a leader. You will never find a king locust. Mind you, they don't seem to need a leader; in fact, they seem to get on very well without one! Locusts fly in great swarms and when it comes to good order, discipline, and working together they're experts, very wise indeed.

The prophet Joel talks a lot about locusts. He says, 'They run like mighty men, they climb the wall like men of war; every one marches in formation, and they do not break ranks. They do not push one another; every one marches in his own column' (Joel 2:7–8). Locusts are like a model army! And because they are so disciplined and united, they are extremely effective. A plague of locusts in one of the Bible lands meant a lot of trouble for the people living there. Joel refers to several different types of locust and the damage they do—'What the chewing locust left, the swarming locust has eaten; what the swarming locust left, the crawling locust has eaten; and what the crawling locust left, the consuming locust has eaten' (Joel 1:4). In a disaster like that God alone could put things right again. Through the prophet Joel, God said, 'I will restore to you the years that the swarming locust has eaten, the crawling locust, the consuming locust, and the chewing locust, my great army which I sent among you' (Joel 2:25).

What do you think God's effective army of locusts can teach us? Surely this—God has another army made up of people called Christians. But where is their leader, their commander? He's nowhere to be seen. Does that mean that Christians are leaderless, like locusts? Certainly not! We can't see him, but the Christian church has an invisible leader, an unseen King of kings, the Lord Jesus Christ.

At times the New Testament depicts the Lord Jesus Christ as a victorious leader, leading a great procession to celebrate his victory. This was something the Romans used to do. When a Roman general was victorious in battle, he was allowed to hold a great victory parade, which was called a triumph. Behind him would march his victorious army, as well as his defeated enemies. When he died on the cross and rose again from the dead, the Lord Jesus Christ won the greatest victory of all time over sin and Satan. The apostle Paul describes Christ's triumphal procession to us—'Having disarmed principalities and powers, he made a public spectacle of them, triumphing over them in it' (Colossians 2:15). Here we see the Lord Jesus Christ in his triumphal procession, leading the wicked spiritual powers he defeated on the cross. But Paul speaks of others in this great procession— 'Now thanks be to God who always leads us in triumph in Christ' (2 Corinthians 2:14). Christians, once the slaves of God's enemy, are now God's army and are always being led by the Captain of their salvation.

There is another important lesson we must learn from the locusts. They are so well disciplined and work so well together that they are very effective in their work. God expects those who are trusting in the Lord Jesus Christ alone for their salvation to behave in exactly the same way. The apostle Paul wrote, 'Let all things be done decently and in order' (1 Corinthians 14:40). He told another church how delighted he was 'to see your good order and the steadfastness of your faith in Christ' (Colossians 2:5). The effect should be far more devastating than even a plague of locusts.

Jesus Christ, the Son of the living God, is the rock of our salvation and he himself said, 'on this rock I will build my church, and the gates of Hades shall not prevail against it' (Matthew 16:18). When some Christians read that verse, they think it means that the church is trying to defend itself against attacks carried out by the gates of hell. But that would have been a strange picture for Jesus to use. Gates don't normally attack people! Think again of the locusts. They don't operate in defensive mode; their way of working is to attack! It's supposed to be the same with the Christian church. By telling other people about the Lord Jesus Christ and by spreading the Christian gospel, Christians are actually attacking the gates of hell and playing their part in rescuing poor sinners who are still held captive by Satan. Are you part of the rescue team or do you still need to be rescued yourself?

It's now time to leave the locusts and to go to our fourth and last small creature, but where you go may depend on which Bible translation you are using. To see the spiders, all we have to do is to stay in the Insect House, but to visit the lizards we have to go across to the Reptile House. Why not have a look at both?

Promotion
The spider [or lizard] skilfully grasps with its hands, and it is in kings' palaces (v.28).

There are many kinds of spiders and lizards in the lands of Bible times. They usually live outdoors, but they can get onto walls and ceilings inside houses. Have you ever found a spider in the bath? Here Agur says that they can be very wise and get into the very best places, even into the palaces of kings! Spiders and lizards belong in deserts, up trees, in swamps or in water, but imagine finding them in a palace! What could be more out of place?

Well, what about a sinner in heaven? It's bad enough when cockroaches, those brown beetles, get into hospital kitchens, which of all places need to be kept spotlessly clean! When talking about heaven the Bible says that 'there shall by no means enter it anything that defiles' (Revelation 21:27). And yet there are going to be sinners in heaven! How can that be?

The answer is that sinners who trust in the Lord Jesus Christ as their Saviour are washed clean from all their sin and covered by the perfect goodness of the Lord Jesus Christ (Revelation 7:14–15). A Christian can say 'It's just as if I'd never sinned.' Jesus said to his disciples, 'In my Father's house are many mansions; if it were not so, I would have told you. I go to prepare a place for you. And if I go and prepare a place for you, I will come again and receive you to myself; that where I am, there you may be also' (John 14:2–3).

When Jesus was crucified, there were two men crucified with him. They weren't what we might call ordinary sinners, but hardened criminals. But one of them asked Jesus to save him and Jesus replied, 'Assuredly, I say to you, today you will be with me in Paradise' (Luke 23:43). This saved sinner was truly promoted to glory. King David was another man who on one occasion in particular was to break God's commandments and commit some terrible sins. And yet he could still say with great confidence, 'I will dwell in the house of the LORD forever' (Psalm 23:6).

We must never make excuses for our sins or say that sin doesn't matter. Sin is a very serious thing; God hates it. On the other hand, we must never forget that God loves sinners and wants to cleanse them from their sin so that they can be with him for ever in heaven. A spider or a lizard in a king's palace doesn't sound right, but it happens! For there to be sinners in heaven doesn't sound right either, but it's a fact. The Lord Jesus Christ came to earth and died on the cross to make it possible.

So there we have Agur's four small but wise creatures. But before we leave them, we'll try to put together the lessons we've been learning. They've taught us about provision, protection, procession and promotion. I'm now going to give you a fifth heading which connects them all together.

Progression

The ants taught us to provide for eternity, the rock badgers showed us where to find protection, the locusts taught us how to behave after becoming Christians and the spiders and lizards reminded us of the eventual goal, heaven itself.

Which stage have you reached? Have you made provision for eternity? If not, let the ants teach you to wake up and take it seriously. 'Seek the LORD while he may be found' (Isaiah 55:6). Have you found protection in the Lord Jesus Christ? If not, let the rock badgers teach you to trust him to be the Saviour who will protect you from your worst enemies. If you've already taken these steps and become a Christian, let the spiders and lizards encourage you to look forward to the day when you will enjoy promotion from earth to heaven to enjoy eternity with your God and Saviour.

But that's in the future. What about the present? How are you getting on in your Christian life? How do you match up to the locusts? Are you playing your part in God's work? Are you a well-disciplined, orderly disciple of the

Lord Jesus Christ? Are you helping others to find him as their Saviour and to grow as Christians? Or are you putting people off and creating unnecessary problems for other Christians?

Whatever stage you've reached, these small but wise creatures have got something to teach you! 'There are four things which are little on the earth, but they are exceedingly wise' (v.24). I hope you don't mind me saying so, but you too are little on the earth! But the question is—are you also exceedingly wise?

Camping

Where do you live? Probably in a house, a flat or a bungalow. In the last chapter we saw where some small animals live. The ants go under the ground and the rock badgers make their home in the rocks, while spiders and lizards sometimes find their way into kings' palaces! That seemed very strange. Sometimes people go to live in some very strange places, too! They leave their nice homes and for a few days go into a field where they put up tents where they can live. It's known as camping and many people enjoy it. Perhaps you do. Some of us couldn't! Even people who say they like camping soon seem to want to come home again to their comfortable beds!

Chapter 11

Actually, whether we like to go camping or not, all of us spend the whole of our lives on earth living in a kind of tent. We know it better as the body. How much do you know about your body? What is it? Why have you got one? Where would you be without it? The Bible gives us the answers and we're going to think about four aspects. The first two are true of everybody, but the last two are true only of those who are trusting in the Lord Jesus Christ as their Saviour.

A tent

According to the Bible the body is not only like a tent, but it is actually a tent itself. What is a tent? Here is a dictionary definition—'Portable canvas shelter stretched and supported by poles and firmly pegged ropes.' If we change a few words we should be able to come up with a physical description of the body. What about this: 'Portable skin shelter stretched and supported by bones and ligaments'? That's what your body is. It's the tent in which you live. Because it's portable, you're able to carry it with you wherever you go. But it's not a permanent fixture. Camping may be fun for a few days, but you might not be so keen on camping if you had to live in a tent day in, day out, year in, year out!

Of course, in Bible times there were people who did live just like that. Abraham lived like a nomad—'By faith he dwelt in the land of promise as in a foreign country, dwelling in tents with Isaac and Jacob' (Hebrews 11:9). If you follow the life of Abraham in the book of Genesis, you will see how he kept moving his tent from one place to another. An Englishman's home is said to be his castle, but Abraham's home was his canvas. We also learn that Abraham's grandson Jacob 'was a mild man, dwelling in tents' (Genesis 25:27).

But even these tent-dwellers were looking forward to the time when they would no longer live in tents on earth, but in a lovely everlasting home in heaven. Abraham certainly was—'he waited for the city which has foundations, whose builder and maker is God' (Hebrews 11:10). When the apostle Peter was approaching the day when he was to die, he wrote about his body as a tent. To his readers he said, 'I think it is right, as long as I am in this tent, to stir you up by reminding you, knowing that shortly I must put off my tent, just as our Lord Jesus Christ showed me' (2 Peter 1:13–14). The tent which was his body was soon going to be taken down. A tent isn't supposed to stay up for ever. The same is true of the body.

Temporary

The body in which you live is not eternal. It's something which has to do with time, it's temporary. The apostle Paul teaches us about this. He's really our biblical expert on tents, because, apart from his service as an apostle and missionary, his occupation was that of a tentmaker (Acts 18:3). To one church Paul made these points about the body—'Our outward man is perishing ...'; 'if our earthly house, this tent, is destroyed ...'; 'we who are in this tent groan ...'; 'While we are at home in the body ...' (2 Corinthians 4:16; 5:1,4,6). We'll complete some of these verses in a minute, but can you see how Paul keeps repeating that the present body is something which doesn't last for ever? Like a tent it can get old or damaged. In the end, either at death or when the Lord Jesus Christ comes again our bodily tents will be taken down.

But what is going to happen after all of that? Will people exist as spirits without bodies? No, says the Bible. Let's complete some of the verses which we've just looked at and we'll see what will happen to Christians. Paul says that the bodily tent will go, but the Christian will be covered by something better, something which will last for ever:

For we know that if our earthly house, this tent, is destroyed, we have a building from God, a house not made with hands, eternal in the heavens. For in this we groan, earnestly desiring to be clothed with our habitation which is from heaven. ... For we who are in this tent groan, being burdened, not because we want to be unclothed, but further clothed, that mortality may be swallowed up by life (2 Corinthians 5:1–2,4).

The bodily tent of the Christian with all its aches, pains and problems will one day be replaced by a perfect heavenly home which will last for ever.

Paul had already told the Corinthian church a lot about this in his earlier letter to them, especially in 1 Corinthians 15, where he spoke about the Lord Jesus Christ. Think about what happened to Jesus after he died on the cross. He was buried, but then he rose again from the dead. Was he a spirit without a body? Certainly not! And yet his body was different. He rose in a body with 'flesh and bones' (Luke 24:39), but in that resurrection body he did things which he hadn't done before, like suddenly appearing in a room despite the doors being locked.

The Bible says that when the Lord Jesus Christ comes again, Christians are going to be raised from the dead as well, not as spirits without bodies, but with perfect resurrection bodies. This is how Paul described the difference between the old body which dies and is buried and the new body which will last for ever—'The body is sown in corruption, it is raised in incorruption. It is sown in dishonour, it is raised in glory. It is sown in weakness, it is raised in power. It is sown a natural body, it is raised a spiritual body' (1 Corinthians 15:42–44).

In another of his letters, Paul sums it all up like this—'For our citizenship is in heaven, from which we also eagerly wait for the Saviour, the Lord Jesus Christ, who will transform our lowly body that it may be conformed to his glorious body' (Philippians 3:20–21). Won't it be wonderful for the Christian to be like Jesus and to have a resurrection body like Jesus?

But what is going to happen to those who do not trust him as their Saviour? It seems that they also will have some kind of resurrection body. The Bible doesn't tell us very much about it, but what it does tell us is very unpleasant. In his Sermon on the Mount Jesus warned people that their whole bodies could 'be cast into hell' (Matthew 5:29–30). On another occasion he said, 'do not fear those who kill the body but cannot kill the soul. But rather fear him who is able to destroy both soul and body in hell' (Matthew 10:28). Jesus also told a story about a man who died and who went to Hades. There this man had eyes with which he could look up and a tongue which was burning hot (Luke 16:23–24). He had some kind of body in which he was suffering for ever. This all sounds very horrible, but remember that it was Jesus who warned us about it.

So the body as we know it on earth is only temporary; it won't last for ever. One day we will all get a resurrection body. But what kind of resurrection body are you looking forward to receiving? So the body is a tent and temporary. Can you think of another word in the Bible which means a tent?

A tabernacle

The body of a Christian is also a tabernacle. That word takes our minds back to the Old Testament when the children of Israel were making their way across the wilderness from Egypt to the land God had promised to give them. He told Moses to construct a special tent called the Tabernacle. This was to be God's tent where God would come and meet his people in a very special way. Just like other tents, it had to be packed up when they were travelling and set up again when they stopped.

The things that were to go on in and around the Tabernacle were to be to God's praise and glory. Many times in the books of Leviticus and Numbers we read about the sacrifices which had to be offered to God at the Tabernacle. The smell from these sacrifices is often described as 'a sweet aroma to the LORD' (Numbers 15:3,7,10,13–14,24). While the Christian is living in a bodily tent on earth, the things done in the body are also to be pleasing to God. Only the Christian can please God; it's impossible for the unbeliever to do it—'without faith it is impossible to please him' (Hebrews 11:6). To begin pleasing God we have to put our faith in the Lord Jesus Christ to be our Saviour.

Sometimes this is described as 'asking Jesus into your life'. When people become Christians, something wonderful happens to the bodily tents in which they live. The Lord Jesus Christ comes to live in them as well by his Holy Spirit. The body is then not only the tent in which the Christian lives, but also the tabernacle where God lives! Is God sharing your tent with you or are you still living on your own? As soon as we start trusting the Lord Jesus Christ as our Saviour we can do the things which please God. Paul told one Christian church that God 'has given us the Spirit. ... we walk by faith, not by sight. ... we make it our aim, whether present or absent, to be well pleasing to Him' (2 Corinthians 5:5,7,9).

The Lord Jesus Christ had a body which was truly human but without sin. The apostle John has an interesting way of describing the life of Jesus on earth—'the Word became flesh and dwelt among us' (John 1:14). Those words can also be translated 'he tabernacled among us', or 'he pitched his tent among us'. We could say that, in order to save us from our sins, the Lord Jesus Christ left his lovely home in heaven and came down to spend some time camping in a tent on earth. His was a perfect tent, because he was God living in a body (Colossians 2:9).

Later, Jesus spoke about his body in an even more wonderful way. He had just driven out of the temple in Jerusalem all the activities which should never have been going on there in the first place. The Jews asked him for a sign to prove that he had a right to take this action. 'Jesus answered and said to them, "Destroy this temple, and in three days I will raise it up." Then the Jews said, "It has taken forty-six years to build this temple, and will you raise it up in three days?" But he was speaking of the temple of his body' (John 2:19–21).

Long before this the Jews had settled in the Promised Land. As they were no longer travelling, they no longer needed a tabernacle to keep on putting up and packing away. Instead God had instructed them to build a temple to serve as his house. In the course of time a series of temples were built and destroyed by their enemies. On this occasion, the Jews thought that Jesus was talking about destroying their temple and putting another building up in a matter of only three days! But he was actually talking about his body; he was going to die and be raised from the dead on the third day. He described his body as a temple; the body of a Christian is also described not only as a tent and a tabernacle, but as a temple.

A temple

God's house is no longer to be regarded as a building. Rather, God is to be thought of as living in his people. The world-wide Christian church is like a temple; the body of each individual Christian is also like a temple. It was again the Corinthian church that received the apostle Paul's teaching on this—'Do you not know that you are the temple of God and that the Spirit of God dwells in you? If anyone defiles the temple of God, God will destroy him. For the temple of God is holy, which temple you are' (1 Corinthians 3:16–17). 'Or do you not know that your body is the temple of the Holy Spirit who is in you, whom you have from God, and you are not your own? For you were bought at a price; therefore glorify God in your body and in your spirit, which are God's' (1 Corinthians 6:19–20). 'For you are the temple of the living God' (2 Corinthians 6:16).

What a great responsibility it is to be a Christian, a member of the church of God. Have you ever realized how important you are to God? If you are a Christian, God actually lives in you by his Holy Spirit. Your body is his temple. You don't belong to yourself. God bought you with the shed blood of the Lord Jesus Christ. Your body is a tabernacle where you should please God and it's also a temple where you should honour God. That should be the aim of the Christian life.

So what is life like in your tent? One way of helping ourselves to please and honour God is to think about the future. We did a little of that earlier, when we saw that the body as the Christian knows it on earth is only temporary. The Christian looks forward to having a resurrection body like that of the Lord Jesus Christ. That should make us want to be like him now. The apostle John says, 'we know that when he is revealed, we shall be like him, for we shall see him as he is. And everyone who has this hope in him purifies himself, just as he is pure' (1 John 3:2–3).

In the last but one chapter of the Bible John gives us some facts about heaven. God is going to live, dwell and 'tabernacle' with his people— 'Behold, the tabernacle of God is with men, and he will dwell with them, and they shall be his people. God himself will be with them and be their God' (Revelation 21:3). And here's a riddle for you. There won't be a temple in heaven and yet there will be a temple in heaven! John says of heaven, 'I saw no temple in it, for the Lord God Almighty and the Lamb are its temple' (Revelation 21:22). We thought about this several chapters ago when we were enjoying a day out. In heaven, Christians will be in the very presence of God. They won't need any kind of building in which to meet.

There's more. They will have lost all the old aches, pains and problems which they used to have to put up with in their old bodily tents on earth! John learns that 'God will wipe away every tear from their eyes; there shall be no more death, nor sorrow, nor crying. There shall be no more pain, for the former things have passed away' (Revelation 21:4). Suffering will play no part in the eternal lives of those who have resurrection bodies like the Lord Jesus Christ.

But those who have never trusted in him as their Saviour will have some kind of body in which they are going to suffer for ever and ever (Revelation 21:8). Jesus came camping among us on earth and died in a body on the cross to save us from that. Make sure that you have put your trust in him; then go on to please and honour him in your body.

On safari!

W e've now reached the last group of things which interested Agur. First came some things which were never satisfied, next some things which were too wonderful for him to understand, then some things which make the earth tremble, and fourthly the small creatures which are small but wise. The final group begins, 'There are three things which are majestic in pace, yes, four which are stately in walk' (Proverbs 30:29). Agur's first and main example of this is 'a lion, which is mighty among beasts, and does not turn away from any' (v. 30).

We're off to the safari park to see the big cats! There's quite a lot about them in the Bible. The leopard is mentioned eight times and there are over 100 references to the lion. You may find that a little strange, because nowadays the lion is an African animal and not one that we associate with Bible lands. However, in those days the lion was found over a much wider area. In recent years London Zoo has concentrated on Asiatic lions, which are now quite rare.

Before we leave for the safari park, we must make sure that our own pets are all right and that they have enough to eat and drink while we're out. Do you have any pets of your own? When I was a boy we always had between one and three cats. There was black and white Billy, tortoiseshell Bunty, black and white Felix, tabby Timmy, two Gingers, tortoiseshell Kitty and a dear little black cat called Cindy who had to be put to sleep in April 1989 at the grand old age of nineteen. While we're on our journey to the safari park, I'd like to tell you a story about Cindy.

In the summer of 1970 she was found on the wall of our back garden, a small black kitten. My family made enquiries but nobody claimed her, so she stayed. One night between the following Christmas and New Year I was upstairs in my bedroom. It was very late and the rest of the family had gone to bed. Cindy was sitting on top of a chest of drawers in my bedroom. Suddenly, she jumped down onto the back of an armchair which tipped backwards under her weight. The legs of the chair crashed back onto the floor, disturbing my uncle in his bedroom directly beneath. I could hear him shouting up the stairs; I was being blamed for all the noise! My immediate reaction was to want to go straight downstairs and to protest loudly that it wasn't my fault at all. It was all the cat's fault! I was really going to lose my temper! But I was stopped in my tracks and I couldn't even leave my bedroom. I couldn't run shouting downstairs. God had spoken to my conscience and had made me aware that, although I wasn't to blame for the noise Cindy had made, I was about to commit a sin by losing my temper. At that very moment God led me to turn my back upon the sin I was about to commit. But that wasn't all. At the very same moment I said to myself, 'So it is true then.' I'd suddenly realized the truth of all I had been taught about God, about the Lord Jesus Christ, and about sin and salvation during the previous four years at the local boys' Bible class. The result was not only that I repented of my sin, but also that I put my faith in the Lord Jesus

Christ to save me from my sin. In one sense I had been led to the Lord by a cat! Even if you don't like cats yourself, can you blame me for liking them?

Sadly we don't have any cats now. They're all dead. It's very sad when pets die. You've looked after them and they've been good company, but they're now missing. Some of our cats died at very strange times indeed. Of our two tortoiseshell cats the first, Bunty, died on a Christmas Day, and the second, Kitty, who was very ill, went out during the early hours of a Good Friday and was never seen again. They really were Bible cats! Of course it's not only small domestic cats that die, but the big cats as well. A man called Eliphaz said to Job, 'The old lion perishes for lack of prey, and the cubs of the lioness are scattered' (Job 4:11). In Psalm 104 the psalmist says a lot about different animals and the way in which God usually provides for them. He says to God, 'These all wait for you, that you may give them their food in due season. What you give them they gather in; you open your hand, they are filled with good. You hide your face, they are troubled; you take away their breath, they die and return to their dust' (vv.27–29).

We've nearly reached the safari park now, but there is time to ask just one question. Why do pets die? Why do animals die? Animals died in the flood. Why? It's all the fault of human beings! Before Adam and Eve sinned against God, nothing died. But when sin entered the world, it affected everything and brought death to animals as well. Pets and other animals die because they are all under the curse that the sin of mankind has brought upon the earth. If they could talk, they could rightly point the paw at us and say, 'This is all your fault!' Well, we're now at the entrance of the safari park and as we go round we're going to learn how sin has affected mankind. The big cats are going to give us three pictures about people and their sin.

The sinner depicted as a restrained leopard

Can the Ethiopian change his skin or the leopard its spots? Then may you also do good who are accustomed to do evil (Jeremiah 13:23).

Just look at the leopards in their enclosure. The leopard is a remarkable animal. It isn't the largest of the big cats, but it's remarkably powerful for its size. The male leopard can kill another creature and carry it up a tree even if it weighs twice as much as he does! Leopards are very agile. They're excellent at climbing and jumping. It has been known for a leopard to make a jump twenty feet long. That may not sound very far, but it's not bad when at the same time it also involves leaping over a railway truck seven feet high! In other words, the leopard can do a combined high jump and long jump at one attempt! It's also a very adaptable animal. Leopards are not fussy eaters. They'll eat anything from a beetle to a zebra. They can do so much. But in one respect a leopard, whether in the wild or in captivity, is totally restricted and restrained, says the Bible. It can't change its spots! They can't be washed off and they can't be scratched off. They're permanent! The leopard is absolutely powerless to do anything about them.

In the verse quoted above, the leopard is compared with us. What can mankind do? Man has a brain and can use it to be very wise and clever. Man has a will; he can be powerful and influence others. Man has a heart and can be brave. Man has muscles and can be strong. Man has a mouth and can speak well. But just like the leopard, men and women have got spots! Not spots on their skin, but spots of sin. We're all born with sin in us; sin is a disease which we catch from our parents. But don't blame them; they caught it from their parents, and it goes all the way back to Adam and Eve, our first parents. From the time we are born we are sinners and as a result we commit sin. As Jeremiah said, we're 'accustomed to do evil'. We've fallen short of God's perfect standards and everything we do is to some extent spoilt by sin. Sin has got into every part of us. The leopard cannot change its spots and we can't do good in God's sight. Because we are sinners, we cannot naturally please God.

Quoting from several psalms the apostle Paul wrote, 'There is none righteous, no, not one; there is none who understands; there is none who seeks after God. They have all turned aside; they have together become unprofitable; there is none who does good, no, not one' (Romans 3:10–12). Many people like to try to turn over a new leaf or to make New Year's resolutions, but in God's sight people are unable to do it. In Jeremiah's verse above, the Ethiopian is stuck with the colour of his skin, which is black, the leopard is stuck with a covering of spots, and people are stuck with the corruption of sin. But there's a big difference. The Ethiopian has no need to change the colour of his skin; he has no need to be ashamed of the skin colour God gave him! The leopard doesn't want to change his spots; they serve as his camouflage and help him to keep out of sight when he's out hunting for his dinner! People don't always want to get rid of their sins, but we desperately need to lose them. Sin doesn't help us in any way apart from giving us a little fun which won't last. Sin is a disaster and 'the wages of sin is death' (Romans 6:23). It gets worse. Having been taught a lesson by the leopard, we're now going to drive into the lions' enclosure and see what the king of beasts can teach us.

The sinner devoured by a roaring lion

Be sober, be vigilant; because your adversary the devil walks about like a roaring lion, seeking whom he may devour (1 Peter 5:8).

A pride of lions is a magnificent sight. As we watch them let's read a few verses about them from the Psalms—'O LORD my God, in you I put my trust; save me from all those who persecute me; and deliver me, lest they tear me like a lion, rending me in pieces, while there is none to deliver' (Psalm 7:1–2). 'He lies in wait secretly, as a lion in his den; he lies in wait to catch the poor' (Psalm 10:9). 'They have set their eyes, crouching down to the earth, as a lion is eager to tear his prey, and like a young lion lurking in secret places' (Psalm 17:11–12). 'My soul is among lions' (Psalm 57:4).

As you can see, the lion is often used as a picture of ferocity and danger. We'd better make sure all the car windows are properly shut! Actually, as a rule, lions are not as dangerous as leopards. They don't usually attack people. But if you come across a rogue lion, a maneater, you're in real trouble! The devil is like that kind of lion. He's a dangerous maneater, and as sinners in his grip we're helpless. Left to ourselves we're easy meat, easy prey for the devil.

But the verse about him being like a roaring lion is followed by others which hold out some hope for us—'your adversary the devil walks about like a roaring lion, seeking whom he may devour. Resist him, steadfast in the faith. ... But may the God of all grace, who called us to his eternal glory by Christ Jesus, after you have suffered a while, perfect, establish, strengthen, and settle you' (1 Peter 5:8–10). The devil, despite being like a roaring lion, can be resisted by people with faith. Peter was writing to Christians. Because they were trusting in the Lord Jesus Christ as their

Saviour, they could resist the devil and survive his attacks. That's something we can't do before we become Christians. The difference between a Christian and a non-Christian when they both are attacked by the devil can be seen clearly if we think about the twelve men Jesus chose to be his apostles. Eleven of them were believers, but one wasn't. The devil attacked the unbeliever, Judas Iscariot, and a believer, Peter, just before Jesus was crucified. See if you can spot the difference.

'Then Satan entered Judas, surnamed Iscariot' (Luke 22:3). The roaring lion took complete control of Judas. It was just as if he had been devoured by the devil. John's gospel describes Judas in the same way when the apostles were eating the Last Supper with Jesus—'And supper being ended, the devil having already put it into the heart of Judas Iscariot, Simon's son, to betray him … Satan entered him' (John 13:2,27). Judas the unbeliever was devoured by the roaring lion. Soon, when he realized that he had betrayed innocent blood, he did a terrible thing. He killed himself.

But the roaring lion also had a go at one of the believers, Simon Peter. Jesus warned Peter that Satan was in fact going to attack all the apostles—'Simon, Simon! Indeed, Satan has asked for you, that he may sift you as wheat. But I have prayed for you, that your faith should not fail; and when you have returned to me, strengthen your brethren' (Luke 22:31–32). Peter soon failed his Lord. He denied him three times, but because Peter was trusting in the Lord Jesus Christ, he survived. The roaring lion, the devil, managed to bite him, but couldn't devour him. If we look back to what Peter later wrote about the roaring lion in 1 Peter 5:8–10, we may well think that he was recalling his own experience. The devil roared, Peter vainly tried to resist, but Jesus restored him. Peter says that what God did for him, he can do for us if we are trusting in the Lord Jesus Christ. When faced by Satan the roaring lion, our only hope of deliverance is God. He alone can rescue the sinner.

There are some good pictures of that in the Old Testament when God protected believers from real lions. They 'through faith … stopped the mouths of lions' (Hebrews 11:33). Think of Samson, the strongman of the Bible—'Now to his surprise, a young lion came roaring against him. And the Spirit of the LORD came mightily upon him, and he tore the lion apart as one would have torn apart a young goat, though he had nothing in his hand'

(Judges 14:5–6). It was the Spirit of God that enabled Samson to survive victorious following that unexpected attack.

When David was about to confront the giant Goliath, he was greatly helped by remembering how God had protected him when wild animals had attacked his flocks of sheep—'David said, "The LORD, who delivered me from the paw of the lion and from the paw of the bear, he will deliver me from the hand of this Philistine"' (1 Samuel 17:37).

And of course, while we are driving around inside the lions' enclosure, we are bound to think of Daniel in the lions' den! What did King Darius discover the morning after Daniel had been thrown into the lions' den? We'll read the whole passage:

Then the king arose very early in the morning and went in haste to the den of lions. And when he came to the den, he cried out with a lamenting voice to Daniel … 'Daniel, servant of the living God, has your God, whom you serve continually, been able to deliver you from the lions?' Then Daniel said to the king, 'O king, live forever! My God sent his angel and shut the lions' mouths, so that they have not hurt me, because I was found innocent before him; and also, O king, I have done no wrong before you.' Now the king was exceedingly glad for him, and commanded that they should take Daniel up out of the den. So Daniel was taken up out of the den, and no injury whatever was found on him, because he believed in his God. And the king gave the command, and they brought those men who had accused Daniel, and they cast them into the den of lions—them, their children, and their wives; and the lions overpowered them, and broke all their bones in pieces before they ever came to the bottom of the den (Daniel 6:19–24).

That's a very exciting account, isn't it? Daniel was protected from real lions by his faith in the living God. The king made a decree that people were to worship this great God 'who has delivered Daniel from the power of the lions' (Daniel 6:27).

In the New Testament, the apostle Paul once felt as if he was in the lions' den. He was on trial at Rome; all his companions had deserted him. No one supported Paul as he was surrounded by his accusers and enemies. But Paul knew that God was with him and he could say 'I was delivered out of the mouth of the lion. And the Lord will deliver me from every evil work and preserve me for his heavenly kingdom' (2 Timothy 4:17–18).

We've spent a long time in the lions' enclosure surrounded by the king of the beasts. It's been very helpful, because we've seen that God not only protected his people in the Old Testament from real lions, but that he can protect us today from people who behave like lions, and especially from Satan who behaves like a man-eating lion. He's the biggest problem. But how does God deliver sinners from the grasp of the devil? Here we're going to see a strange sight. Having safely got out of the lions' enclosure, we can at last get out of the car and walk across to a fenced enclosure. The attached label informs us that inside this enclosure is another lion, but what do we see when we look? Not a lion, but a lamb! What's going on here?

The sinner delivered by a ransoming lamb

In his vision which we know as the book of Revelation, the apostle John saw a scroll sealed with seven seals. Nobody was worthy to break the seals and open the scroll. John was very upset. He tells us what happened next—'one of the elders said to me, "Do not weep. Behold, the Lion of the tribe of Judah, the Root of David, has prevailed to open the scroll and to loose its seven seals"' (Revelation 5:5). When he spoke about the Lion of Judah, this elder in heaven was talking about the Lord Jesus Christ. Can you imagine how encouraged John must have been and how eagerly he looked to see the Lion of Judah?

But he goes on to tell us that he had a big surprise—'And I looked, and behold, in the midst of the throne and of the four living creatures, and in the midst of the elders, stood a Lamb as though it had been slain' (v.6). John saw the Lord Jesus Christ looking not like a splendid lion, but like a sacrificed lamb! As the sacrificed lamb the Lord Jesus Christ was worthy to open the scroll and its clips. In the book of Revelation we read no more about the Lion of Judah, but we keep on reading about the Lord Jesus Christ as the Lamb. The Lion and the Lamb are the same person, the Lord Jesus Christ. The lion is the king of beasts and the Lord Jesus Christ is the King of Heaven, the great King of kings. But he left heaven and came to this world to act as the Lamb and be sacrificed on the cross so that sinners could be ransomed and saved.

It's not what we would expect! Imagine that you are being attacked by a maneating lion. To your rescue comes a lamb! What can a lamb do for you?

You'd rather see a man with a gun in his hand! But the lamb catches the attention of the lion. Instead of continuing its attack upon you, the lion goes after the lamb. The lamb is taking your place and sacrificing its life so that you can escape and survive. That's exactly what the Lord Jesus Christ has done for sinners. He became a sacrificial lamb in order to face Satan, the roaring lion, in our place.

What a perfect replacement he is for us! As sinners we are depicted as restrained leopards. We're spotted by our sin and unable to get rid of the marks. The Lord Jesus Christ is pictured not as a spotted leopard, but as a spotless lamb. The apostle Peter wrote that we can be brought back to God only 'with the precious blood of Christ, as of a lamb without blemish and without spot' (1 Peter 1:19). Jesus had no sin; he was spotless. He took our spots, our sin, upon himself so that he could suffer instead of us and save us.

As sinners we are in danger of being devoured by Satan, the roaring lion. But Satan has been diverted. As a result he tried to devour the spotless Lamb. He tried to make Jesus sin, but failed and left him alone for a while with the intention of attacking him again later. Satan entered Judas Iscariot so that he could get Jesus arrested and put to death. Jesus let it happen. When he was arrested, he said, 'this is your hour, and the power of darkness' (Luke 22:53). On the cross, the Lord Jesus Christ was exposed to the punishment of all our sin and his heavenly Father turned away from him.

Hundreds of years before this, King David wrote a psalm which foretold what was going to happen to Jesus upon the cross. It begins with that terrible cry that Jesus was to make—'My God, My God, why have you forsaken me?' (Psalm 22:1). Then it shows how Jesus faced the attacks of his enemies and it includes this verse—'They gape at me with their mouths, like a raging and roaring lion' (Psalm 22:13). This was bound to include, above all, his biggest enemy, the devil, who 'walks about like a roaring lion. seeking whom he may devour' (1 Peter 5:8). The person the devil most wanted to devour was the Lord Jesus Christ. Can you see how perfectly Jesus has taken the place of sinners?

There's one more stage. As sinners we can be delivered only by a ransoming lamb. But listen to what happens later in Psalm 22. These are the prophesied thoughts of Jesus on the cross—'Save me from the lion's mouth' (Psalm 22:21). The Lamb himself was crying to God for deliverance. But it was only when the Lord Jesus Christ had taken our place, suffered for our sins and finished all that had to be done to save us, that he himself was delivered from his terrible suffering on the cross. At that very point Psalm 22 brightens up and looks forward to the Lord Jesus Christ rising from the dead with the good news that sinners can be saved from their sins and enjoy eternal life.

It's time to leave the safari park. While we're on our way home I want you to think over what the Bible says about you. You are a sinner, cut off from God, and you can't do anything about that yourself. Satan, the roaring lion, has got you. But there's a greater lion, the Lion of Judah, the Lord Jesus Christ. He became like a lamb and was put to death on the cross for your sin. If you trust him as your Saviour and ask him to forgive you for your sins, you'll be ransomed by the Lamb and rescued from the roaring lion.

The best animal for you to remember from our visit to the safari park is not the leopard or the lion, but the lamb. Do what John the Baptist told people—'Behold! The Lamb of God who takes away the sin of the world!' (John 1:29). Look to the Lord Jesus Christ and let him take away your sin.

Howzat! A day at the cricket

We've come across some very unusual things in Proverbs 30, but nothing perhaps as strange as Agur's last saying—'For as the churning of milk produces butter, and wringing the nose produces blood, so the forcing of wrath produces strife' (v.33). Somewhere among all of that it sounds as if an argument has turned into a fight and someone has got punched on the nose! A Christian ought not to get into a punch-up with anyone! And yet the Christian life itself is a battle; to help us understand something about the Christian battle we're going to think about my favourite sport, cricket, which has produced many famous sporting battles for over more than 100 years. We'll get down to the cricket ground early, well before start of play. That will allow us to find our seats and settle down.

The background

Cricket has had many connections with the Christian faith. Some Christians have been outstanding cricketers. In the early days of international cricket, the England team sometimes included two of three Christian brothers with the surname Studd. C.T. Studd and his brother George both played for England against Australia. In fact, C.T. Studd made his debut for England during 1882 in a match later known as the 'Ashes' match. Studd didn't score a single run and Australia won a close match by just seven runs. The defeat came as such a shock to people in England that one of the newspapers made out that English cricket had died and that its ashes would be sent to Australia. Later, a wooden bail was burnt and its ashes were put into an urn. This is still kept in the museum at Lord's cricket ground in London, but whenever England and Australia play a series of test matches, the winner of the series is said to have won the Ashes.

To get back to the Studd brothers, they had been greatly helped by having a father who had become a Christian in 1877 as the result of hearing the great evangelist D.L. Moody preaching. Soon after that the three brothers had become Christians on the same day as one another! After a period when his Christian life hadn't been going very well, C.T. Studd took several of his fellow England cricketers to hear Moody preach and at least two of them, including the England captain, became Christians. In later years they prayed regularly for C.T.Studd when he gave up his cricketing career to become a missionary, first in China, then later in Africa.

Another famous England cricketer was the late David Sheppard. From 1950 to 1963 he played on and off for England with greater success than C.T. Studd and was twice England captain in 1954. His test match career was regularly interrupted because he wanted to concentrate on his work as a minister. Later he became Bishop of Woolwich, then of Liverpool.

Other cricketers were prepared to stand out when they were expected to play cricket on the Lord's Day. As far back as 1930, the great England batsman Sir Jack Hobbs created quite a stir in India when he objected to being asked to play on a Sunday. As a result the tour he was on had to be rearranged. One church minister said in his sermon, 'Good old Jack! He never played a straighter bat than that!' More recently in 1971 two New Zealand cricketers, Bruce Murray and Vic Pollard, both Christians, refused to play in a test match against England because the match was to include play on a Sunday. Vic Pollard had been the New Zealand vice-captain in 1969. By taking this stand he probably gave up his opportunity of ever becoming captain. In 1973 I had the privilege of meeting him at the Oval cricket ground in London, during New Zealand's next tour of England. Vic Pollard had come on the tour on the understanding that he would not play in any match which included playing on a Sunday. On one Sunday while his colleagues were playing, he was to be found preaching in a church in another part of London! For all these men being a Christian was more of a priority than being a cricketer.

It has even been suggested that cricket began as a picture of the Christian faith! Many years ago *The Christian Herald*, a weekly newspaper, contained a letter from a reader about the origins of cricket. The writer said that in the Middle Ages it was called 'cryce'—'The three stumps represented the Trinity. This wicket was guarded by eleven monks in turn representing the faithful apostles. Armed with sticks, they defended the kingdom of heaven against the devil, another monk who bowled a wooden ball at the stumps.' Whether that's all true or not, I don't know.

But cricket is a good picture of the Christian life. The apostle Paul used to refer to Olympic sports like boxing and athletics in his letters to churches as illustrations of the Christian life and I think he might well have written about cricket as well if it had been played in his time. He did, however, write to the church at Ephesus about the Christian battle, and used the picture of a Roman soldier to illustrate it. We're going to use that passage to see how cricket can teach us about the Christian life. Well, we've said enough about the background and the match is about to begin.

The battle

Be strong in the Lord and in the power of his might. Put on the whole armour of God, that you may be able to stand against the wiles of the devil. For we do not wrestle against flesh and blood, but against principalities, against powers, against the rulers of the darkness of this age, against spiritual hosts of wickedness in the heavenly places. Therefore take up the whole armour of God, that you may be able to withstand in the evil day, and having done all, to stand (Ephesians 6:10–13).

Has anybody told you not to get too excited when you are playing a sport? They may have said, 'You mustn't take it too seriously. After all, it's only a game.' But that's not as easy as it sounds. Nobody likes losing; you'd rather win! There have been some notable cricketing battles. As we've mentioned already, series between England and Australia are known as 'the battle for the Ashes'. A match between the county teams of Yorkshire and Lancashire is called 'the Roses Match', in memory of the real battles during the English Wars of the Roses between the Yorkists and Lancastrians in the fifteenth century.

If you're a Christian, some people may tell you not to take being a Christian too seriously. But the Christian life is a battle. It has to be taken seriously. Think of the batsman alone at the wicket. As he faces the bowling he's outnumbered by his opponents. He stands alone at one wicket, while around him hover the whole of the opposing team, eager to get him out. They're all against him, the opposing captain, the bowler, the wicket-keeper and the eight other fielders. Their aim is to bowl him out, to catch him out or to run him out, to get him out in one way or another. Some left-handed men mentioned in Judges 20:16 would have made wonderful fielders!

The Christian faces such a battle. The devil is like the opposing captain and he has a team of evil powers and spirits under his command. They want to get you out. We need to know something about our opponents. How will they attack us? The batsman needs to know how they are likely to play, what tactics they will use and what tricks they may have up their sleeves to try against him. Christians need to know exactly the same about our spiritual enemy, the devil. To one church the apostle Paul expressed his concern 'lest Satan should take advantage of us; for we are not ignorant of his devices' (2 Corinthians 2:11). Let's see what our opponent's tactics are. We'll be able to observe some of them as we watch the match.

The bowler

Put on the whole armour of God, that you may be able to stand against the wiles of the devil ... above all, taking the shield of faith with which you will be able to quench all the fiery darts of the wicked one (Ephesians 6:11,16).

Bowlers come in many different styles, but there are two main categories, seam and spin, or, to be more simple, fast and slow. Most bowlers tend to be one or the other, though a few, like the great West Indian Gary Sobers, could do both. The devil can come at us in all kinds of different ways. At the start of the innings the captain will almost always ask his fast bowlers to bowl. So we'll watch them at the start of the match.

The quickest bowlers have been able to send the ball down at not far short of 100 miles per hour! Their aim will be to get the batsman out by sheer speed. Sometimes when you watch a fast bowler, you may be forgiven for thinking that he's trying to knock the batsman out! Some fast bowlers have been given some wonderful nicknames. In the Australian side against which C.T. Studd played was a man called Spofforth, who was actually known as 'the demon bowler'! In more recent times we've had others like Fiery Fred (Trueman) and Terror Thomson. These bowlers and many others like them have caused a lot of trouble to batsmen. Sometimes there have been some very nasty accidents and cases where the batsman has ended up 'retired hurt'.

The devil sometimes comes at us like this. In Ephesians 6:16 we read about 'the fiery darts of the wicked one'. He's aiming them at us! In the early 1930s, the English fast bowler Harold Larwood was instructed by his captain to bowl at the bodies of the Australian batsmen to make it hard for them to score runs. This form of bowling was quickly nicknamed 'bodyline bowling' and it worked well, but after some serious injuries to their batsmen the Australians complained that the English team was behaving as if it was a war, not a game. When Satan attacks us, it really is war. We discovered that in the previous chapter—'Be sober, be vigilant; because your adversary the devil walks about like a roaring lion, seeking whom he may devour' (1 Peter 5:8). At times like this Satan comes at us without any disguise—he uses sheer brute force.

As the innings proceeds there will come a time when the captain will give his fast bowlers a rest and ask his spin bowlers to take over. The spin bowler may look so slow and harmless, but in the right circumstances and on the right kind of pitch he can get the ball to fly up at the batsman too. There are different kinds of spin bowlers. So that we don't get too confused, I'll only describe spin bowlers who bowl with the right arm. Imagine that you are a right-handed batsman. An off-spin bowler will make the ball spin off the pitch from your right to your left. A leg-spin bowler will make the ball spin from your left to your right. Or he may be able to bowl a ball called a googly—from the way it comes out of his hand, you'd expect it to spin from your left to your right, but when it hits the pitch it goes the other way instead! Sometimes when the ball is spinning well, spin bowlers can tie up batsmen in all kinds of knots. The batsman doesn't know what's going to happen next. One of the very best bowlers of this kind in recent years was a left-hander, Derek Underwood. His nickname was 'Deadly'!

Ephesians 6:11 refers to 'the wiles of the devil', his evil schemes. He uses all kinds of tricks to try to deceive us. Sometimes he will attack us like the googly bowler, coming at us in disguise and doing the opposite of what we expect. To a church which was getting deceived in many ways, the apostle Paul said, 'Satan himself transforms himself into an angel of light' (2 Corinthians 11:14). A Christian wouldn't expect to suffer any harm at the hands of an angel of light, so it would be very dangerous if Satan came up disguised like one. Perhaps you wouldn't expect a friend, a relative, a nice person or a religious person to lead you astray, but they can all be the very kinds of people whom Satan uses to lead Christians astray.

Let's remind ourselves of the bowler's aim. He's attacking the batsman to get him out. Satan attacks the life of the Christian. But in some forms of cricket, where the batting side has only a limited time in which they are allowed to bat, the bowler's main aim may be a defensive one—to keep the batsmen as quiet as possible and to make it very hard for them to score many runs.

Sometimes Satan uses that method against the Christian. We're supposed to be telling others about the Lord Jesus Christ, but to stop us showing others the way out of Satan's kingdom, the devil simply tries to keep us quiet. The apostle Paul was aware of this problem. At the end of our passage in Ephesians 6:19–20 he made a request that his readers would pray 'that utterance may be given to me, that I may open my mouth boldly to make known the mystery of the gospel, for which I am an ambassador in chains; that in it I may speak boldly, as I ought to speak.' Satan doesn't always strike the Christian; sometimes he will be content if he can silence us.

We've looked so far at the background, the battle and the bowler. Now we must take time to watch the one who is going to be our picture of a Christian.

The batsman

Therefore take up the whole armour of God, that you may be able to withstand in the evil day, and having done all, to stand. Stand therefore, having girded your waist with truth, having put on the breastplate of righteousness, and having shod your feet with the preparation of the gospel of peace; above all, taking the shield of faith with which you will be able to quench all the fiery darts of the wicked one. And take the helmet of salvation, and the sword of the Spirit, which is the word of God (Ephesians 6:13–17).

Like the bowler (and indeed like a soldier) the batsman may sometimes be defensive and sometimes on the attack. At times he may have to bat very defensively and grimly, determined to keep his wicket at all costs in the face of everything the opposing bowlers may throw at him. The opening batsmen very often have to do this. If they can wear the bowlers down and tire them out a bit, the later batsmen may find it much easier to attack the bowling later. The batsman must be determined to stand firm. Sometimes the Christian has to concentrate on defence against the devil. 'Resist him, steadfast in the faith' (1 Peter 5:9). Just as a soldier is protected by his armour, the batsman is protected by his equipment, and the Christian also needs protection to be able to stand against the devil. Let's concentrate now on the batsman as he faces up to the bowling.

Do you see the pads on the batsman's legs? How do they stay on? They're kept on properly by means of pad-straps. If the straps aren't done up properly, they'll flap loose or fall off and the batsman will be in difficulties. The Christian needs something to hold everything else together. To do that God has given us truth. To become Christians we need to know a certain amount of truth—that God is perfect, that we are sinful, that Jesus is the Son of God who died for our sins and that we can be forgiven and saved when we trust in him alone. We learn all this from God's Word, the word of truth. The devil is a liar and we must have the truth to be able to stand up against him.

Especially when he's facing the fast bowlers, the batsman may expect some short-pitched bowling aimed at his body and may well wear a chest-protector, otherwise he may get hit over the heart, which could be very painful and dangerous. The Christian needs something to protect his heart, and for that purpose God gives us righteousness. But whose righteousness? The Christian always needs to think like this—'I'm not righteous. I'm a sinner. But Jesus died on the cross to take away my sin and to give me his perfect goodness in return. I'm trusting in what he has done, not in what I do. When God looks at me, he doesn't see my sin, but the perfect goodness of the Lord Jesus Christ.' If we pretend that we're righteous in our own goodness, Satan will find it easy to attack and defeat us. But he can never damage the perfect goodness of the Lord Jesus Christ. That can protect us.

The bowler and opposing side will always hope that the batsman may slip when going for a run. It will then be easier to run him out. If the batsman is wearing unsuitable footwear, he will be in danger of slipping. But our batsman is wearing proper cricket boots which grip the surface of the ground properly. They will help him to keep standing on his feet. The Christian also needs something to keep him steady and to prevent the devil from tripping him up. To achieve that, God gives us peace. The Christian is no longer at war with God. Already he has got peace with God. But there's another kind of peace. If the Christian remembers to thank God and to trust God when problems come, he can know the peace of God. Instead of falling into great distress and despair, the Christian can keep going calmly, steadily and firmly even when in great difficulties.

We've mentioned the batsman's pad-straps. The pads themselves are very important to protect his legs. They're like a second line of defence. Used properly they can get in the way. The ball can thud into them and do no more damage. If he takes them off, the batsman risks getting some very nasty bruises and even a broken leg. The Christian also needs an additional line of defence. It's faith—faith in God's promises, whether they have to do with the forgiveness of our sins or the meeting of our needs. It's when the Christian forgets God's promises that he or she begins to have doubts—that's like taking the pads off. If we do that, we'll get hit.

Since about 1980 nearly every batsman in first-class cricket has batted in a helmet. Batsmen used to wear caps or no headgear at all. But fast bowling has got more and more hostile and after many injuries to batsmen, it was realized that something was needed to protect their heads. The Christian also needs a head-protector. Our minds need protecting. For that purpose God has given us the hope of salvation. The devil likes to make Christians think that they have lost their salvation. He tries to take away their joy in their salvation. That can be lost as the result of sin or lack of prayer or Bible-reading or lack of Christian fellowship. God has given us 'as a helmet the hope of salvation' (1 Thessalonians 5:8). Many batsmen became more confident as the result of wearing a helmet. That's also true of the Christian who holds onto the hope of salvation.

We've seen that batting can be defensive. The aim is to stand. But the real point about batting is that it's supposed to be attacking. The main aim should be to score. We mustn't forget the last vital item of equipment. What's that in the batsman's hand? It's his bat! The bat is his instrument for scoring runs and for getting the better of the bowler, even to knock him out of the attack. Soldiers not only defend; they also attack. The Christian also has an attacking weapon, the word of God. That really wounds the devil. When Jesus was tempted by the devil in the wilderness, he made use of the word of God. With it he knocked the devil out of the attack and the devil had to leave him (Matthew 4:1–11).

As Christians we don't have the power to do that by ourselves. The power to do that lies in the word of God. You'll never see a batsman hit a six with his hand. Even if he could do it, he'd end up with a broken hand and several broken fingers! The power of the batsman is in his bat. I remember once batting in a house match at school. It was a limited-overs match and I wasn't doing at all well. After being in for some time, I'd only scored a run or two. Then I played a shot which I can't explain. The bowler was quite fast and I went to play the ball defensively a few yards to my right. The next thing I knew was that the ball was soaring high in the sky way over the bowler's head and into the distance. Eventually it landed far away in the tennis courts! I've tried to hit a six like that on many occasions, but probably never as far and as high as that unintentional shot! It must have been timed perfectly, but the power was in the bat. I hadn't put any power whatsoever into the shot. Sometimes as Christians we feel very weak and powerless against the attacks of the devil. We feel helpless. But it's amazing what a weak Christian can do simply by trusting and using the word of God. The power is not in us; it's in God's word.

The batsman will need to speak to his captain to get his advice and help. Usually his captain will be an experienced cricketer who's been through it all before. The Lord Jesus Christ is the captain of our salvation. After describing the armour, the apostle Paul says that the Christian should pray 'always with all prayer and supplication in the Spirit, being watchful to this end with all perseverance and supplication for all the saints' (Ephesians 6:18). We need to keep in touch with our captain by prayer, both for ourselves and for other members of our team, the Christian church. The Lord Jesus Christ has been through it all before. He's used the equipment perfectly against every kind of temptation and he can help us to make a good score. Every run that the batsman makes gets recorded in the scorebook and everything that the Christian does in God's service is recorded in heaven. One day it will be rewarded. But some cricketers never learn to bat properly. They have to stay down at number eleven. Don't be the kind of Christian who doesn't learn how to use God's Word and the protection God provides.

I hope you've enjoyed our day at the cricket ground. The game of cricket has a lot to teach the Christian. But I must check whose side you are on. Are you in the right team, God's team? Have you owned up to God about your sin? Have you admitted to him that he would be right to punish you for it? Have you trusted in the Lord Jesus Christ to save you and forgive you, because he died on the cross for you? If not, you're still in the devil's team. You've not yet got the truth. You've got no righteousness, no peace, no faith and no hope of salvation. In the end, the devil and all who are on his side are going to lose the battle. Change sides while you've still got time. A game of cricket has to end at close of play. The opportunity to get right with God has to end at the close of life. Make sure you join God's team; then you'll be on the victory side.

Finale—music and the Bible

D o you enjoy music? Most people like to listen to music of one kind or another. Perhaps you play a musical instrument; my instrument is the piano. We've seen that Agur had many interests but as far as we can tell from Proverbs 30, he doesn't appear to have had any interest in music at all. Perhaps he was unmusical, or even tone deaf! We don't know. But what we do know is that there is plenty about music in the Bible, so for our final outing we're going to visit the concert hall. First we'll take a general look at the Bible and let it give us a music lesson.

The place of music—where it's found

Although there is nothing about music in Proverbs 30, there are over 600 references to music in the Bible. We won't be looking at them all! Music can be found in the Old Testament and in the New Testament, in Genesis, the first book of the Bible, and in Revelation, the last book of the Bible. It can be heard on earth and in heaven, in joy and in sadness. So we discover in the Bible victory songs, and music at feasts, festivals and marriages, but also at funerals. The wicked made music; of them Job said, 'They sing to the tambourine and harp, and rejoice to the sound of the flute' (Job 21:12).

But the people of God made music as well. The Bible includes a songbook known as the book of Psalms. Out of the 150 psalms, nearly half are believed to have been written by King David, who was known as 'the sweet psalmist of Israel' (2 Samuel 23:1). One of David's leading singers was a man called Asaph, who wrote another twelve of the Psalms. A much later king of Judah, Hezekiah, was very keen on their songs—'King Hezekiah and the leaders commanded the Levites to sing praise to the LORD with the words of David and of Asaph the seer. So they sang praises with gladness' (2 Chronicles 29:30).

David had a very musical family. His son, King Solomon, wrote two of the Psalms and we're told that he wrote over a thousand songs (1 Kings 4:32). Another of the books in the Bible is Solomon's Song of Songs. And we shouldn't forget Moses. He wrote Psalm 90, and two of his songs are to be found in the first five books of the Bible, which he wrote. The very last book of the Bible talks about people making music in heaven, playing harps and singing 'the song of Moses, the servant of God, and the song of the Lamb' (Revelation 15:2–3).

You can see from that reference that Bible music includes both choral singing and instrumental playing. The Psalms often refer to singing 'a new song' and they were written to be sung. Some churches make a special point of singing the Psalms today. Actually the word 'Psalms' comes from a Greek word meaning 'twanging of harp strings'. The book of the prophet Habakkuk ends with this instruction—'To the Chief Musician. With my stringed instruments' (Habakkuk 3:19). It's like a kind of psalm. In case you think this is all to do with the Old Testament, this is what the apostle Paul wrote in Colossians—'Let the word of Christ dwell in you richly in all wisdom, teaching and admonishing one another in psalms and hymns and spiritual songs, singing with grace in your hearts to the Lord' (Colossians 3:16). He wrote something very similar in Ephesians, which we'll look at later.

Back in the Old Testament we can find a long list of all the instruments in King David's orchestra, together with the names of the singers and instrumentalists as well as the conductor and choirmaster (1 Chronicles 15:16–28). The whole passage is interesting to read, but here are some extracts—'David spoke to the leaders of the Levites to appoint their brethren to be the singers accompanied by instruments of music … Chenaniah, leader of the Levites, was instructor in charge of the music, because he was skilful' (vv.16,22).

Biblical musical instruments are divided into three main sections—strings, wind and percussion. We find the following in the Bible, though you may find that some are called something different, according to which Bible translation you use:
- Strings—harp, lute, lyre, psaltery
- Wind—brass, flute, horn, trumpet
- Percussion—bells, cymbals, tambourine, timbrel

Put them all together and you've assembled quite an orchestra. Most of the references to these instruments are found in the Old Testament, but the apostle Paul made a point of mentioning a few of them when writing 1 Corinthians. In the last few chapters we find him referring to the sounding brass and a cymbal (13:1), as well as the flute, harp and trumpet (14:7–8). The trumpet appears again in 15:52. I think you'll agree that music is quite a big subject in the Bible. We've seen enough to gain some background knowledge. The next question to ask is—where did music start? Where did it come from? Who, as it were, gave birth to music?

The parentage of music—where it's from

We don't have to read very far into the Bible before we come across the first mention of music in connection with a man called Jubal, who 'was the father of all those who play the harp and flute' (Genesis 4:21). He seems to have been the first man to have played an instrument. From this, music appears to have had a man as its inventor. Since then both men and women have become famous as singers and instrumentalists, but strangely enough all the famous composers happen to have been men! But was music really invented by a man?

Towards the end of the book of Job, God addressed Job with questions similar to some of the things Agur asked in Proverbs 30:4. But note the additional reference to music—'Where were you when I laid the foundations of the earth? Tell me, if you have understanding. Who determined its measurements? Surely you know! Or who stretched the line upon it? To what were its foundations fastened? Or who laid its cornerstone, when the morning stars sang together, and all the sons of God shouted for joy? (Job 38:4–7).

According to this, the concept of music was present when God created the world! Did you know that the Bible actually talks about God himself singing? That must sound wonderful. What would make God sing? Here's the answer—'The LORD your God in your midst, the Mighty One will save; he will rejoice over you with gladness, he will quiet you with his love, he will rejoice over you with singing' (Zephaniah 3:17). When people are saved and become God's people, God rejoices with singing!

We know from what the Lord Jesus Christ said that the angels of God rejoice when a sinner turns back to God (Luke 15:10); all heaven rejoices with them (Luke 15:7). Jesus also told a story about a boy who left his father and got into a lot of trouble. He might as well have been lost and dead. When he eventually came back to his father, there was much rejoicing, and music played a part in the great celebrations (Luke 15:25). That's a picture of the way in which God rejoices when somebody becomes a Christian. It would appear that he sings for joy. Have you given the angels something to sing about? Have you come back to God the Father through faith in the Lord Jesus Christ? Have you made God sing for joy?

But to go back to our original question—who invented music? I think we have to say that God himself did. The apostle Paul says, 'For of him and through him and to him are all things' (Romans 11:36). God is the creator of everything, including music. The great Reformers of the past, like Luther and Calvin, knew this. Martin Luther said that music was a gift of God, not a gift of men. John Calvin believed music to be one of the main things God had given man to enjoy.

Some years ago I enjoyed reading a book called *The gift of music; great composers and their influences* (Crossway Books, 1987) by two ladies, Jane Stuart Smith, who used to be an opera singer, and Betty Carlson. I'm going to repeat some of the things that great composers said about their music; though not necessarily all Christians, these composers had a clear idea of the relationship between God and the gift of music. When Haydn (1732–1809) was applauded during a performance of his oratorio *The Creation*, he said, 'Not from me. It all comes from above'. He meant that God, not man, was the giver of music. Following the success of his *New World Symphony*, Dvorak (1841–1904) said, 'May God be thanked'. He could see that his ability to compose music was 'The gift of God'.

So when we think about music, we should realize that God is its true father. 'Every good gift and every perfect gift is from above, and comes down from the Father of lights' (James 1:17). Music has come from God. But why do we have music?

The purpose of music—what it's for

Here the apostle Paul's words in Romans 11:36 will be of great help again— 'For of him and through him and to him are all things, to whom be glory forever.' Music didn't start on earth; God created it. It came from God and it exists for us to give praise and glory back to God.

When Moses and the Israelites escaped from the Egyptians across the Red Sea, they used singing to thank God. They 'sang this song to the LORD, and spoke, saying, "I will sing to the LORD … The LORD is my strength and song, and he has become my salvation"' (Exodus 15:1–2). Several times, mainly in the Psalms, we read things like 'sing to the LORD a new song!' Psalms 96, 98 and 149 begin like that.

But it wasn't only singing that was to be used for God's glory. Of the Levites, who helped the priests in the work of the Old Testament Temple, 'four thousand praised the LORD with musical instruments, "which I made," said David, "for giving praise"' (1 Chronicles 23:5). The Levites had a part to play when King Solomon had the Temple dedicated to God. They took their positions 'with instruments of the music of the LORD, which King David had made to praise the LORD' (2 Chronicles 7:6). If you read Psalm 150, you'll see that it's all about praising God with all sorts of musical instruments. Again, when the Temple was dedicated to God, we read that 'the trumpeters and singers were as one, to make one sound to be heard in praising and thanking the LORD … they lifted up their voice with the trumpets and cymbals and instruments of music, and praised the LORD' (2 Chronicles 5:13).

Whenever you sing or play an instrument, do you remember to do it for God's glory? He's given the gift of music to us as well as the ability to sing or play. The apostle Paul spoke of this in a very interesting way when he wrote to the church at Ephesus. He told them to 'be filled with the Spirit, speaking to one another in psalms and hymns and spiritual songs, singing and making melody in your heart to the Lord' (Ephesians 5:18–19). The last phrase could be translated, 'singing and playing on a stringed instrument in your heart to the Lord.' Even if you can't sing nicely and even if you can't play any musical instrument, you can still sing and play to the Lord in your heart. He can hear, even if nobody else can.

A little earlier we saw that some of the great composers believed that their gift of music had come from God. Many composers have gone on to say that music should be used to praise and glorify God. Andreas Werckmeister (1645–1706), who was an organist, called music 'a gift of God to be used only in his honour.' Bruckner (1824–1896) dedicated his ninth and last symphony 'to the good Lord'. Stravinsky (1882–1971) said that 'Music praises God' and also dedicated his *Symphony of Psalms* to the glory of God. They weren't just talking about hymns and other church music. Everything in the life of the Christian should glorify God, not only what we do and say in a church service. Even the ordinary music we like to hear should cause us to thank God for it.

As we saw, John Calvin said that music is a blessing that God has given to us. It can help us and we can enjoy it. In the Old Testament there were occasions when music was used to comfort people who were in distress. King Saul suffered from an evil spirit which tormented him. His servants decided that he would be comforted if he could sit and listen to someone playing the harp well (1 Samuel 16:16–17). The shepherd-boy David was an excellent harpist and was employed to play to Saul. Whenever Saul was tormented, 'David would take a harp and play it with his hand. Then Saul would become refreshed and well, and the distressing spirit would depart from him' (1 Samuel 16:23).

On another occasion, Jehoshaphat, the good king of Judah, had got mixed up with the bad kings of Israel and Edom. They found themselves in deep trouble and asked God's prophet Elisha to give them God's word. Elisha was obviously very annoyed about the whole situation and seems to have been in such a state that he needed to listen to a musician playing to help him calm down before he could share God's word with the kings (2 Kings 3:15). Nowadays some ministers find it very helpful to sit down and listen to some music when they are getting ready to think about what they are going to preach at church. This helps them to relax. The great preacher Dr Martyn Lloyd-Jones found that the music of Mozart (1756–1791) helped him in this way. If music does us good and if we can truly thank God for the beauty of the sounds we hear, it's a very good thing indeed.

But we need to be careful. Sometimes music can be unhelpful, especially when it has words set to it, as in a song, or when it accompanies acting, as in an opera or a ballet. It's good to ask questions about the music we hear. If it's a song, are the words sinful? If it's an opera or ballet, does it tell a rude story? If it's a hymn or piece of religious music, does it say things about God or the way we can be saved which are different to what the Bible teaches? We can't really thank God for music like that and perhaps it would be better not to listen to it.

Music can be misused just as easily as the other things that God has given us. Just as we use music in church, so music gets used in false religions. We should avoid that kind of music. King Nebuchadnezzar of Babylon had a great statue erected and this is what everybody was ordered to do—'at the time you hear the sound of the horn, flute, harp, lyre, and psaltery, in symphony with all kinds of music, you shall fall down and worship the gold image that King Nebuchadnezzar has set up' (Daniel 3:5). You'll remember that when the band started to play, everybody bowed down to worship the idol, except for three godly men who refused to do so. It wasn't that they didn't like the music; they couldn't go along with the idolatry with which it was being associated. They insisted on obeying God's commandments and God honoured them for taking such a brave stand.

But centuries earlier, in fact just after God had given Moses the Ten Commandments, God's people, the Israelites, themselves made a golden calf to worship. When Moses came down from the mountain, he found the people singing and dancing as they worshipped the idol they had made. He was furious (Exodus 32:18–19). They were sinning against God and music was helping them to sin. That's one way in which music can be misused.

But there's a much easier way to misuse music. God has given us so many blessings. But many people enjoy the things God has given them without thanking him or even thinking of him. They take the gift and ignore the giver. People do that with music. Listen to what some of God's prophets said. Firstly Isaiah—'Woe to those who rise early in the morning, that they may follow intoxicating drink; who continue until night, till wine inflames them! The harp and the strings, the tambourine and flute, and wine are in their feasts; but they do not regard the work of the LORD, nor consider the operation of his hands' (Isaiah 5:11–12). They had music at their parties, but no thought for God. Have you been to parties like that? Perhaps it would be better not to go.

Another prophet, Amos, said something similar. He complained about people who at their parties played instruments like King David, but who, unlike David, had no concern for God's people (Amos 6:4–6). What do you think God has to say about their music? We're actually told how he feels about the religious music of his people when their lives are displeasing to him. God said, 'Take away from me the noise of your songs, for I will not hear the melody of your stringed instruments' (Amos 5:23). Do you ever misuse God's gift of music? Or do you enjoy music without having any thought of God? Music has come from God. We should thank him for it and use it to praise and honour him.

Music should bring glory to God and so should the whole life of the Christian. What effect does your life have? There are some kinds of music which I can't enjoy. Some sounds are terrible! I remember once going to a children's concert at the Royal Festival Hall in London. The programme was very good, except for one piece which was written for about thirty percussion instruments. For several minutes one percussionist charged around the platform crashing and banging those instruments. There was no melody, no harmony; it was just a terrible din. Why mention it? Because it's possible for the Christian's life to be like that. The apostle Paul wrote, 'Though I speak with the tongues of men and of angels, but have not love, I have become sounding brass or a clanging cymbal' (1 Corinthians 13:1). The passage goes on to say that if we don't have love in our lives, it doesn't matter what else we do or say; it all counts for nothing. It doesn't help anybody. Have you received God's love? Are you passing it on to others?

We've seen where music started and why we have it. Finally we're going to consider what is going to happen to music in the future.

The prospects for music—what's its future?

There is music in heaven now and there will be music in heaven throughout eternity! In the book of Revelation it's very clear that God is always going to be praised for saving sinners. John first saw the heavenly beings praising the Lord Jesus Christ, 'each having a harp … And they sang a new song' (Revelation 5:8–9). Later on he heard the sound of the saved—'And I heard a voice from heaven, like the voice of many waters, and like the voice of loud thunder. And I heard the sound of harpists playing their harps. They sang as it were a new song before the throne' (Revelation 14:2–3). Still later, John saw God's victorious people 'having harps of God. They sing the song of Moses, the servant of God, and the song of the Lamb' (Revelation 15:2–3). Then in chapter 19, John was almost deafened by the sound of the great Hallelujah chorus in heaven. Are you going to be one of those joining in? You will be if you've trusted in the shed blood of the Lord Jesus Christ to cleanse you from all your sin.

But before all of God's people are reunited in heaven, there's going to be one last special musical event, immeasurably greater than that great English tradition, the Last Night of the Proms. On the last day, when the Lord Jesus Christ comes again, there will be a last great trumpet-blast. The apostle Paul wrote, 'For the trumpet will sound, and the dead will be raised incorruptible, and we shall be changed' (1 Corinthians 15:52). That will be a great day for Christians, when God gathers them into his presence.

But the last trumpet will have a different meaning for those who don't know the Lord Jesus Christ as their Saviour. One of the Old Testament prophets foresaw it—'The great day of the LORD is near; it is near and hastens quickly. The noise of the day of the LORD is bitter; there the mighty men shall cry out. That day is a day of wrath, a day of trouble and distress, a day of devastation and desolation, a day of darkness and gloominess, a day of clouds and thick darkness, a day of trumpet and alarm' (Zephaniah 1:14–16).

While heaven is filled with forgiven people singing joyful songs of praise to their Saviour, the only music to be found in the mouths of the unsaved in hell will be everlasting weeping and wailing. What tune will you be singing in eternity? Don't wait until the last trumpet to find out. There's another trumpet which you can listen to now. It's the gospel trumpet, which tells people about their sins and the way they can be saved from sin (Isaiah 58:1; Ezekiel 33:1–6). If you've read through this book, you will have heard that trumpet many times. I trust that it has been blown clearly. Have you heard the message loud and clear? Then come to Jesus! Come today!

My book of hobbies and God's book, the Bible